FIFTY YEARS' EXPERIENCE OF PIANOFORTE PLAYING • OSCAR BERINGER

Publisher's Note

The book descriptions we ask booksellers to display prominently warn that this is an historic book with numerous typos, missing text, images and indexes.

We scanned this book using character recognition software that includes an automated spell check. Our software is 99 percent accurate if the book is in good condition. However, we do understand that even one percent can be a very annoying number of typos! And sometimes all or part of a page is missing from our copy of a book. Or the paper may be so discolored from age that you can no longer read the type. Please accept our sincere apologies.

After we re-typeset and design a book, the page numbers change so the old index and table of contents no longer work. Therefore, we often remove them.

We would like to manually proof read and fix the typos and indexes, manually scan and add any illustrations, and track down another copy of the book to add any missing text. But our books sell so few copies, you would have to pay up to a thousand dollars for the book as a result.

Therefore, whenever possible, we let our customers download a free copy of the original typo-free scanned book. Simply enter the barcode number from the back cover of the paperback in the Free Book form at www.general-books. net. You may also qualify for a free trial membership in our book club to download up to four books for free. Simply enter the barcode number from the back cover onto the membership form on the same page. The book club entitles you to select from more than a million books at no additional charge. Simply enter the title or subject onto the search form to find the books.

If you have any questions, could you please be so kind as to consult our Frequently Asked Questions page at www. general-books.net/faqs.cfm? You are al-so welcome to contact us there. General Books LLC™, Memphis, USA, 2012. ISBN: 9780217831840.

❧ ❧ ❧ ❧ ❧ ❧ ❧ ❧

HARVARD COLLEGE LIBRARY
, FROM
M 7. *2* r rTHE BEQUEST OF
'EVERT MNSEN WENDELL 18)8 piE JOY-AL CADEMY OF jJUSIC Tenterden Street, Hanover Square.
Instituted, 1822. Incorporated by Royal Charter, 1830.
Patron:
HIS MOST GRACIOUS MAJESTY THE KING.
President:
  H.R.H. THEDUKE OF CONNAUOHT & STRATHEARN, K.O.
Principal:
SIR ALEXANDER CAMPBELL MACKEN-ZIE,
Mus.D, LL.D., D.C.L., F.R.A.M.
THE ROYAL ACADEMY OF MUSIC offers to Students of both sexes (whether amateur or professional) a thorough training in all branches of music under the most able and distinguished Professors. In addition to receiving individual lessons, Students have the advantage of attending the Orchestral, Choral, and Chamber Music Classes, and the weekly lectures on music and musicians. Evidence of their progress is given at the Fortnightly and Public Concerts, and by periodical Operatic Performance.

A large number of Scholarships and Prizes are founded and are competed for periodically.

METROPOLITAN EXAMINATION.

An Examination (independent of Academy teaching) of Musical Composers or Performers, and Teachers, is held twice a year in London, viz., during the Academy Summer and Christmas Vacations. Successful Candidates are created Licentiates of the Royal Academy of Music, with the exclusive right to append to their names the initials L R. A. M.; and receive diplomas to the effect that they are judged to be fully qualified for the branches of the musical profession in which respectively they have been examined. The Syllabus is issued annually at Easter.

Prospectus and Syllabus obtainable on application to

F. W. RENAUT, Secretary.

OP THE ROYAL ACADEMY OF MUSIC and ROYAL COLLEGE OF MUSIC FOK LOCAL EXAMINATIONS IN MUSIC.

Patron-HIS MAJESTY THE KING. President—H.R.H. THE PRINCE OF WALES, K.G. Associated Board. William E. Bioqe, Esq., Chairman. Hon. Q. W. Spencer Lyttelton, C.B., Deputy-Chairman. Sir Alexander C. Mackenzie, Mus. doc, St.Andr., Cantab, et Edin., LLD., D. C.L, Principal of R.A.M. Sir C. Hubert H. Parry, Bart., C.V.O., M A, Mus.Doc, Cantab., Oxon. et Dublin, D.C.L, LLD., Director of R.C.M., &c, &c. Auditor—Sir Lesley Probyn, K.C.V.O.

Syllabus A.-LOCAL CENTRE EXAMINATIONS.

Theory Examinations held at all Centres in March and November. Practical Examinations at all Centres in March—April, and the London District and certain Provincial Centres in November—December also.

Syllabus B.-SCHOOL EXAMINATIONS.

These Examinations are arranged in circuits, and are held during three periods, as follows: (a) March, April; *(b)* June, July; and (c) October, November.

The Examinations are open to all Schools and Teachers in the United Kingdom, who are at liberty to select any or all of the above periods for Examination.

Specimen Theory Papers set in the Local Centre and School Examinations of past years can be obtained on application, price 3d per set per year, post free.

The Subjects for Examination under Syllabus A and B are comprised in the following list:— Primary Theory. Pianoforte. Viola. Harp. Rudiments ofMusic. Organ. Violoncello. Wind Harmony. Violin. Double Bass. Instruments.

Counterpoint. Singing.

The Board offers Six Exhibitions for competition annually, open to candidates who qualify in the Local Centre Examinations, and otherwise fulfil the requirements detailed in Syllabuses A and B. These Exhibitions entitle their holders to two or three years' free tuition at the Royal Academy of Music or the Royal College of Music.

Syllabuses A and B, entry forms, and any further information will be sent, post free, on application to: —

Telegrams:—"Aisocia, London."
JAMES MU1R, Secretary.

Telephone 7356 Gerrard.! Bedford Square, London, W.C.

CHAPTER I. INTRODUCTORY. IN looking back over a fifty years' experience of pianoforte-playing and teaching the fact that stands out most vividly in my recollection is the enormous progress made all over the world, but more particularly in England, during the 'sixties and 'seventies of the last century. I say "more particularly in England" advisedly, for it must be confessed that this country stood at that time in more urgent need of musical progress than any other of the leading nations of the world. All the more honour to her and to her musicians for having wiped off the arrears so handsomely, and for winning her present proud position amongst the foremost of her rivals!

In submitting the facts of this progress to a brief review, I am afraid that the personal pronoun must inevitably crop up now and again, as the period of that improvement happens to coincide with my own musical growth, and I was therefore lucky enough to come into personal contact with nearly all the great pianists of that time, including Moscheles, Liszt, von Billow, Rubinstein, Tausig, and the rest of that glorious band of artists to whom the credit of raising the standard of pianoforteplaying throughout the world is chiefly due.

I made my first public appearance in 1857 at the Crystal Palace as an infant prodigy, giving daily recitals, as well as playing with the orchestra two or three times a week—an engagement which lasted for the best part of nine years, almost without a break.

Although the Crystal Palace concerts were admittedly the best in England after the Philharmonic and Musical Union concerts, my solo-programmes there were a medley of terribly mediocre music. I had to play Kuhe, Dohler, Alfred Jaell, Osborne, Ascher, Brinley Richards, and Thalberg, whose *Home, Sweet Home* became a nightmare to me through constant repetition, while the only compositions of Liszt that I played were his *Rhapsodie No. 2* and some of his operatic Fantasias. These, together with a sprinkling of *Lieder ohne Worte*, and an occasional Nocturne or Waltz of Chopin, formed my entire repertoire.

I also played duets there with my elder brother Robert, including various operatic arrangements, arrangements of overtures, some of Schubert's Marches, and other music of the same description.

With the orchestra I played the Rondos of Hummel, the D minor Concerto of Mozart, the Concertos and Caprice of Mendelssohn, some of Moscheles' works, and, later on, Beethoven's 1st and 3rd Concertos. The most prominent pianists living at that time in England were Arabella Goddard, Charles Halle, Ernst Pauer and Lindsay Sloper. I had every opportunity of hearing them all, and for a long time their playing was my only instruction. I am not certain, however, that I did not gain more in this way than by taking lessons, which were then of the most perfunctory character, as I quickly found out when I was able to afford them. The method, even of the best teachers, was primitive: one was either praised to the skies, or told that the piece wanted more practice: in the latter event the usual prescription was an hour's scales and a dose of Czerny's *Etudes de la Velocite* or Cramer's Studies, to be taken as many times a day as the poor sufferer could stand it — and this was all! As for any proper finger or touch training, such things did not enter the head of the pianoforte-teacher of those days. Could your instructor play, he or she would play the piece over to you, and if you were keen you tried to copy them. Looking back to that date, I often envy the young people of the present day, Who have the opportunity afforded them of being systematically trained from the very beginning, whilst we poor beggars had to pick up the crumbs of knowledge where and how we could.

Still more enviable, perhaps, were the teachers of that time. What a delightfully easy task they must have had! No L. R. A. M., no A. R. C. M., no, not even an Associated Board, to disturb their slumbers and interfere with their digestion! The word "slumbers" brings to my mind a story that I can vouch for, of one of the bestknown teachers of the 'sixties, who was addicted to a quiet nap during his lessons. Two mischievous sisters, pupils of his, noticed this failing, and played him the following trick. The one whose lesson came first waited till the worthy man was comfortably off, and then stole out of the room on tiptoe, her sister as quietly taking her place and going on playing. The teacher woke up shortly afterwards and said, "Yes, that'll do. Very good! Now go and fetch your sister." I will leave you to imagine the shock the poor man's nerves received when his pupil sweetly answered, "Please, *I'm* the sister"!

My first experience in teaching was in 1859, and as I had rather a good opinion of myself I made up my mind to charge is. 6d. a lesson; but, alas! I had overrated my earning capacity, for the mother of my first pupil beat me down to is. 3d. This was the harder to bear at that particular moment, as my pride was only just recovering from a nasty knock it had received at one of the Opera Concerts at the Crystal Palace. Madame Titiens, the great dramatic soprano, was singing there, and happened to say in my hearing that she was very thirsty: I jumped up and got her a glass of water, and she, seeing a small boy in a short jacket, not unnaturally thought that a half-crown would be acceptable to him, and offered me one, with some smiling words. My feelings cannot be described. I drew myself up to my full 4 ft.

2 in., and said in a voice quivering with outraged dignity, "No thank you, I am the Solo Pianist of the Crystal Palace." A peal of laughter from Madame Titiens hurt me still further, and I don't believe that the kiss she proceeded to give me quite healed my wounded pride.

I remember receiving another gift, which caused me no end of gratification. Queen Marie Amelie, the wife of Louis Philippe, who was, of course, quite an old lady at the time, used frequently to come to the Palace concerts, and one day she sent an equerry with a purse and a bag of sweets as a present for me. When I learnt that they were from the Queen of France I was immensely impressed, and I remember the severe internal struggle I had as to whether I should eat the sweets or keep them as a souvenir. I am sorry to say that greed prevailed over veneration— but they were very *good* sweets!

The following press criticisms written with reference to Wagner and his operas form a striking commentary upon the lack of musical intelligence which was so painfully apparent during the early 'fifties. They were written by the foremost English critics of the period, and were reprinted by *The Musical Courier,* June 25, 1896. Though not dealing with our specialized subject— the pianoforte— they show so clearly the remarkable difference between the opinions held on musical subjects at that time and the views that obtain at the present day, that their admission into these pages may well be pardoned. They are headed "Wagner's Press Notices,London, 185 5," and run as follows:

"We hold that Herr Richard Wagner is not a musician at all... This excommunication of pure melody, this utter contempt of time and rhythmic definition, so notorious in Herr Wagner's compositions (we were about to say Herr Wagner's *music),* is also one of the most important points of his system. It is clear to us that Herr Wagner wants to upset both opera and drama... He, Wagner, can build up nothing himself. He can destroy, but not re-construct. He can kill, but not give life... What do we find in the shape of Wagnerian 'Art Drama'? So far as music is concerned, nothing better than chaos, 'absolute' chaos.... Look at *Lohengrin*—that *'best* piece'; Your answer is there written and sung.. . It is poison —rank poison... This man, this Wagner, this author of so many hideous things—and above all, the overture to *Der Fliegende Hollander,* the most hideous and detestable of the whole—this preacher of the 'future', was born to feed spiders with flies, not to make happy the heart of man with beautiful melody and harmony... All we can make out of *Lohengrin* is an incoherent mass of rubbish, with no more real pretension to be called music, than the jangling and clashing of gongs, and other uneuphonious instruments."—*The Musical World.*

"Richard Wagner is a desperate charlatan, endowed with worldly skill and vigorous purpose enough to persuade a gaping crowd that the nauseous compound he manufactures has some precious inner virtue, that they must live and ponder yet, ere they perceive... Anything more rambling, incoherent, unmasterly, cannot well be conceived. Scarcely the most ordinary ballad writer but would shame him in the creation of melody, and no English harmonist of more than one year's growth could be found sufficiently without ears and education to pen such vile things."—*Sunday Times.*

"The overture to *Tannhauser* is one of the most curious pieces of patchwork ever passed off by selfdelusion for a complete and significant creation. The instrumentation is ill-balanced, ineffective, thin, and noisy."— *Athenaeum.*

It was not only in England that these bitter attacks on Wagner were rife; the musical critics of the whole world rose as one man against him, and it was not till many years later that Wagner came to his own as the greatest dramatic composer the world has ever seen.

I think I have shown pretty clearly the backward state of things musical in the 'fifties: little or no progress was being made, and the few shining examples to the contrary were cried down on all sides. But underneath this superficial stagnation a leaven was fortunately working, which was shortly to ferment the whole mass, and to create a healthy musical activity which has steadily increased from that day to this.

As far as England was concerned I found a most notable improvement on my return in 1866 from Leipzig, where I had gone for two years' study. Brief as my absence had been, a progress little short of miraculous had been made in pianoforte-playing and teaching alike.

The Crystal Palace Saturday Concerts were now firmly established in the popular favour, and regularly every Saturday there was a pilgrimage of music-lovers to this shrine of orchestral music. The Monday 'Pops' were also extremely well patronised, and in addition, pianoforterecitals were just beginning to find favour.

A propos of the Monday Pops, one of the daily papers said:— 'The appellation of popular concerts was originally, in fact, a misnomer. The music given was of the most consistently wwpopular character. Most speculators would have either altered the name of the entertainment or modified the selection of the compositions performed: Mr. Chappell took a bolder course—he changed the public taste."

Professor Ella, who was the first to introduce analytical programmes in England, was also doing good work with his Musical Union Chamber Concerts. These were held at the St. James' Hall, where Ella insisted on having a low platform placed in the centre of the room for the performers, with the audience seated in a circle all round Personally, I found this a most uncomfortable arrangement, and on one occasion it nearly proved my undoing. I had just started playing Chopin's Scherzo in B minor, when my eye was caught by a lady at the further end of the piano, who was evidently badly afflicted with St. Vitus' dance; at any rate, the poor creature was making the most fearful grimaces. Good heavens! I thought, I mustn't look at her, or my memory will go. But do you think I could get away from that face? Not for a moment! It seemed to exert an hypnotic fascination upon me, so that my eyes returned again and again to it, in spite of all I could, do to resist the fatal influence. How I got through without a breakdown I don't know, but get through I did, though in a cold perspiration and with shattered nerves.

To Charles Halle is due the credit of popularising Beethoven's Sonatas in England. He was constantly playing one or othen of them at the Popular Concerts, and was the first artist in England to play all the Sonatas at a series of Beethoven recitals.

In pianoforte-*teaching* an equal improvement was noticeable. Men like W. H. Holmes, Walter Macfarren, Lindsay Sloper, Frederick Westlake, Harold Thomas, Arthur O'Leary, Franklin Taylor, Dannreuther, Fritz Hartvigson and others, were.doing excellent work, and raising the standard of amateur performance to a much higher level.

Amateur ambition had hitherto not soared above the playing of such wishy-washy stuff as Badarzewska's *Maiden's Prayer* (some bars of which are reproduced at the end of this chapter), Ascher's *Alice, Where Art Thou?, La Pluie des Perles,* by G. A. Osborne, and *Warblings at Eve* by Brinley Richards, who was also responsible for *Warblings at Dawn:* for the rest of the twenty-four hours he was dumb. The melodies of all these pieces were of a childishly sentimental description, and were harmonised almost entirely in the tonic, dominant, and sub-dominant, while their modulations were bald and obvious in the extreme.

Now, however, a change had come over the spirit of the amateurs' dream. Throughout the country they were showing an appreciable tendency to play a better class of music. The most popular piece now was the *Sonata Pathetique* of Beethoven, with his *Moonlight Sonata* running it a close second; next in favour was the same composer's Opus 26 in A flat; while of shorter and lighter pieces Mendelssohn's *Rondo Capriccioso*, and three of Chopin's works, to wit the *Valse* in D flat, the *Nocturne* in E flat, Opus 9, and the *Fantaisie Impromptu* in C$ minor, were all prime favourites. The less ambitious were content with such pieces as Rubinstein's *Melody* in F, Grieg's *Norwegian Wedding March,* Litolff's *Spinnerlied,* and other compositions of the same class.

CHAPTER II. SOME COMPOSERS OF THE LAST HALF-CENTURY.

'HE aphorism "Every country has the government that it deserves" might with equal truth be altered to "Every country has the *music* it deserves." With music as with everything else, demand and supply go hand-inhand; and so it was not until the English taste altered for the better, thus creating a demand for music of a higher class, that composition and execution alike began to show distinct signs of improvement. This spirit of progress was particularly pronounced in the early 'sixties, and was marked by the rejection of the ultra-sentimental trash which had hitherto found such favour, and by the adoption in its stead of two particular dance forms, which at this time came into vogue—the *Tarantella* and the *Gavotte.* Every pianoforte composer who could (and a great many who could *not),* wrote and published them, and it was by a Tarantella that Sidney Smith first made his name. Smith, who soon afterwards stepped into Brinley Richards' shoes as the most popular composer of pianoforte music of England, modelled his style on Thalberg's compositions. But while Thalberg's works were decidedly difficult, Sidney Smith had the knack of writing pieces that sounded very brilliant, but which really were comparatively easy to play. His melodies were written on much broader lines than those of Brinley Richards and Badarzewska, while his passage-work was more brilliant, and his modulations showed infinitely greater variety. The *Harpe Aeolienne* was the most popular of his compositions.

Another composer, but of quite a different calibre, to gain popularity at this time was Stephen Heller, a Hungarian living in Paris, whose music was first introduced into England by Charles Halle. Curiously enough, Heller, like Smith, made his first big success with a Tarantella, which became the rage amongst the English amateurs of that period. His musicianship was of a much higher order than Smith's: he wrote 'Studies' which have become standard works, and are widely and deservedly used down to the present day, though his larger works, amongst which I remember four pianoforte Sonatas, are now quite forgotten.'

The Tarantella, which is a South Italian dance in 6-8 time and in quick movement gradually increasing in speed to the finish, has a very interesting origin. The bite of the LycosaTarantula, a spider of great size and malignancy, which at one time infested Southern Europe, used to produce a kind of hysteria, for which this violent form of dancing was the only known cure. In the fifteenth, sixteenth, and seventeenth centuries bands of musicians used regularly to perambulate Italy in order to cure this disease by making the patient dance until he fell down from sheer exhaustion: and in course of time the name of the spider was given to the dance.

The craze for Tarantellas was equalled by that for Gavottes, and each played an honourable part in the musical education of English amateurs, which was now progressing steadily, if slowly. To the Gavotte-fever one important result may be attributed, that through it people were gradually led to an interest in and knowledge of Bach's compositions.

The publishers began to look for Gavottes high and low, and made the important discovery that Bach had written a great many. They proceeded to publish them wholesale, with an eagerness that was attributed by the censorious to the fact that they were non-copyright.

It was at this time that Gilbert made his celebrated *bon-mot* about Bach. An equally ignorant and gushing lady asked him if Mr. Bach had been writing any more of his charming Gavottes lately: to which Gilbert replied, "No, madam, Mr. Bach no longer composes, he *decomposes*!"

The Gavotte was a dance of French

origin written in common time and commencing on the third beat of the bar. Its originality as a "danse grave" lay in the fact that the dancers lifted their feet from the ground, while in former dances of this order they only walked or shuffled. It was practically unknown in England until a French composer named Henri Ghys made a big success with one which had originally been written for Louis XIII., and which he had transcribed for the piano. This had an immense vogue at the time, and may still be heard on the bands at the seaside and in the parks.

The works of F. Edward Bache were the next step in the upward progress of pianoforte compositions, of which he wrote many that were on a far higher level than those of the composers I have just mentioned. His music possessed more charm and poetic feeling, and showed considerably better musicianship. Unfortunately he died, at the early age of twenty-five, in 1858.

Sterndale Bennett, who was a disciple of Mendelssohn, is another of the English composers of that time who deserves honourable mention. His compositions were chiefly remarkable for 'their 'symmetry of form, graceful melody, and brilliant and in many cases original passage-work, but they are sadly lacking in vigour and breadth.

First and foremost amongst the foreign pianoforte composers of that period stands Johannes Brahms, whose compositions are a happy combination of the classical and romantic schools. To Schumann belongs the credit of having been the first to recognise Brahms' genius, and the first piece to make his reputation in this country was his arrangement of Gluck's Gavotte from *Armida,* which was played here for the first time by Madame Schumann. When he visited Schumann in 1843 to show him some of his manuscripts, he had scarcely finished playing the first piece before Schumann called out to his wife, "My dear Clara, you must come and hear this glorious music, such music as you have never heard before." Ten years later Schumann wrote an article in the *Neue Zeitschrift fiir Musik,* in which he

said:—"He came, a stripling over whose cradle the Graces and Heroes had watched. Sitting at the piano he began to discover wonderful regions to us: we were all drawn into his magic circle. He played Sonatas that were really veiled Symphonies, Songs whose poetry one could understand without ever hearing the words, smaller pianoforte pieces of the utmost fascination and charm, and others again that were nothing short of demoniacal."

It is, perhaps, not generally known that Brahms excelled as a player as well. In this regard Schumann wrote of him, "His playing showed the hand of a genius: he could turn the instrument into a full orchestra, swelling from the softest sounds of melancholy to the most triumphant shouts of jubilation." In later years Biilow once said to me, "Had Brahms kept up his practice he could have put us all into his pocket; we should not have had a ghost of a chance against him."

Brahms, like Biilow, could be very sarcastic, and many an anecdote is related of his pungent wit. Biilow used to say that when he sat next to Brahms, he felt like a babe in swaddling-clothes!

The French artist, Saint-Saens, who is happily still living, has also had considerable influence as a pianoforte composer and player. His works are, perhaps, more remarkable for their novelty of effect and clever combinations than for any great inspiration. They show the influence of his extensive travels, for he has consistently endeavoured to implant into his compositions the local colour of the various countries which be has visited, a result which he has most successfully achieved. He is certainly one of the most versatile musicians it has ever been my good fortune to meet. There is no *genre* of music to which he has not applied his hand, generally with success, while as a musical critic he wields a terribly sharp pen.

Although Antonin Dvorak, the Bohemian composer, has not exerted much influence as a writer for the pianoforte, he merits a place in these pages if only on account of the essentially *national* quality of his works, which possess this

characteristic to an even more marked degree than do those of Grieg and Tschaikowsky. Even in his American Symphony, into which he embodies several negro melodies, he every now and then betrays his Bohemian origin, while such works of his as *Die Slavische Tanze, Bilder aus dem Bdhmer Wald,* and his Waltzes and Legends, are one and all instinct with Bohemian rhythm and colour.

Dvorak first came to England in 1884 and stayed at my house for more than a month. He was rather a disconcerting guest to entertain, as he was a true Bohemian in more senses than one. He used frequently to get up at six o'clock in the morning and go out for a stroll with a friend of his, who was also unable to speak a word of English, and I was always on tenterhooks lest they should be landed in some awkward predicament. However, no very serious contretemps occurred, though they found themselves in one or two ridiculous situations. I shall never forget one of their escapades. They had lost their way one fine morning and, feeling hungry, they looked out for a cafe. Dvorak caught sight of some men sitting at a window reading the papers, and said, "Ahl this must be a cafe." They entered, and found a gorgeouslyattired porter in the hall, but, nothing daunted, they went into the room where the men were reading the papers and told the uniformed waiter to bring them some coffee. They were trying hard to make themselves understood, when a gentleman informed them in French that it was not a cafe but the Athenaeum Club, of which he was the secretary. They did *not* get their coffee! refers to it in the following terms:—"At the Albert Hall the conditions were decidedly against Herr Dvorak. The ears of the audience had been somewhat fatigued by the encores accepted during an admirable performance of Mr. Barnby's Leeds Psalm, *The Lord is King.* Dvorak's *Stabat Mater* was not commenced very much before ten, and as after ten Albert Hall audiences have acquired a happy knack of dispersing, the steady exodus which set in could hardly have had the effect of inspiriting a nervous *debutant.* That nervousness was doubtless increased by the fact that one of the most homely and unpretentious of musicians had never before conducted so big a choir and orchestra, nor had appeared before so great an audience. Moreover, he seemed at times wrapped up in his own music, thinking little of his forces, and beating the measure below the music-desk, where only the front rows of the choir could possibly see the *baton.* Nor can the Albert Hall be considered the best place in the world wherein to listen to a composition like Dvorak's setting of Jacopone's hymn. In so vast a space many of the details, of a work full of detail, must necessarily be lost."

Dvorak's principal appearances in this country were at the Albert Hall, the Philharmonic, and the Crystal Palace Saturday Concerts. I had to attend most of the rehearsals to interpret for him, and to express his thanks to the performers, as he was much too nervous to be able to make a speech, even in German. At the Philharmonic he had promised to accompany some of his songs, and had rehearsed them with the singer, but unfortunately his nerve failed him at the last moment, and he said, "It's no good, Beringer, you must play them"—and play them I had to, a task I did not relish in the least, as they were very difficult, and of course I had had no rehearsal.

This nervousness of his detracted greatly from his success over here. The *London Figaro* of March 22, 1884,

Peter Ilitsch Tschaikowsky, the Russian composer *par excellence,* also displayed a strongly national tendency in his compositions, the rhythm of which is essentially Russian, while most of his melodies, if not actually based on national songs, at least portray many of their characteristics. His work has achieved a wonderful vogue in this country, his Concerto in B flat in particular having been played in public more frequently than any other recent work of the same description, while many of his smaller pieces, such as his *Chanson Trisle,* his *Troika-Fahrt,* and many of his waltzes, have become universally

popular. His music generally bears the impress of a Slavonic temperament, now fiery and unrestrained, now melancholy and despairing. He was fond of strong rhythmical effects, sudden contrasts, and unexpected modulations. His death at a comparatively early age was the more sad in that his work was showing consistent improvement, his last compositions being unquestionably the best. and very dapper in appearance. On account of his fatness he had to sit at a considerable distance from the keyboard, and he looked for all the world like a sleek black cat scratching the keys; but the cat was an amiable one that never showed its claws, for his touch was always of the most velvety description: but while his finger-work was excellent, he was sadly lacking in power, and although he played Chopin's waltzes and mazurkas quite charmingly, his rendering of Beethoven or any big works was somewhat wanting in spirit and force. Of later performers Pachmann, to my mind, shows most resemblance to Jaell.

This chapter would not be complete without a reference to Edward Grieg, the Norwegian composer, who has been the most popular composer of pianoforte music in England for the last thirty years. His compositions, like those of Dvorak and Tschaikowsky, are distinctly national in their conception, and bear constant witness to his Scandinavian origin, nearly all his themes being reminiscent of Danish, Swedish, or Norwegian Volkslieder. His *Lyrische Stücke, The Norwegian Wedding March, Humoresken,* and many others of his compositions have achieved a popularity in this country unequalled by the works of any other modern composer.

Since writing the foregoing the deeply regrettable news of this talented musician's death has reached me. On September 4th, 1907, Edward Grieg passed peacefully away, at the age of sixty-four. Born in 1843, he was a fellow-student of mine at Leipzig, where he studied under Hauptmann and Richter for counterpoint, Rietz and Reinecke for composition, and Moscheles

for pianoforte-playing.

CHAPTER III. SOME PIANISTS OF THE SAME PERIOD.

O attempt anything like an exhaustive review of the pianists of this period is quite beyond the scope of this little handbook: a short summary of a few of the most popular native and foreign artists appearing at this date before the English public is all that its limits will allow me.

The most prominent English pianist at this time was Arabella Goddard, a pupil of Kalkbrenner, Thalberg, and Davidson, who was the musical critic of the *Times,* and whom she married in i860. She made her first appearance in England in 1853 at one of the Quartette Concerts, playing Beethoven's Sonata Opus 106 for the first time in England.

I have a very distinct and pleasant recollection of her. She was a very handsome woman, tall, and with perfect pianoforte hands. Her technique was excellent, especially in scales and arpeggi: her octaves, however, were by no means so good, as she played them all with far too rigid a wrist and arm. She used to play the operatic Fantasias of Thalberg almost to perfection, a special favourite of hers being his *Mose in Egitto.* In the interpretation of that style of music she was quite at her best, for though she played classical works very correctly, there was no warmth of expression in her rendering of them. She was one of the first pianists to play solos from memory, although with orchestra she always played from notes,

I need not dwell long upon the playing of Charles Halle, his public appearances having continued down to a comparatively recent date. His style was very like that of Arabella Goddard, and, like her, he was lacking in warmth and depth of expression; but in the matter of phrasing and general musicianship he was greatly her superior. The high standard set by these two artists was hardly maintained by Ernst Pauer and Lindsay Sloper.

The most prominent among the foreign pianists who appeared in England at this date were Thalberg, Rubinstein, Alfred Jaell, Madame Schumann, Ernst

Liibeck, Moscheles, and Ritter, the last named hailing from Paris. All these were to be heard in the late 'fifties or early 'sixties, and all with one exception met with an equally hostile reception from the English press, led by the redoubtable Davidson, musical critic of the *Times*. If to the crime of being a foreigner the artist added the enormity of displaying the slightest modernising tendencies, no matter how great the improvement effected, he or she was absolutely certain to be cut to ribbons by the outraged newspapers. The *Times* on one memorable occasion actually said, "If you want to be shown how *not* to play the piano, go and hear Rubinstein. " Madame Schumann was treated nearly as badly, and for a long time Arabella Goddard reigned supreme according to the *Times* and the press generally. For some reason or other Thalberg managed to avoid the censure of the papers, and was lucky enough to meet with fair treatment at their hands. He appeared in England in 1862 and gave his farewell concert in 1863. His compositions, which are now all but forgotten, had an enormous success at the time, and have made their influence felt down to the present day, to a degree which we, I think, are inclined to under-estimate.

It may perhaps be interesting to pass in review some of the conflicting opinions held with regard to Thalberg by the great musicians of his time. Schumann says that Thalberg kept him in a certain tension of expectancy, not on account of the platitudes which were sure to come, but on account of the profound manner of their preparation, which warns you always when they are to burst upon you. "Thalberg," Schumann continues, "deceives you by brilliant hand and finger work in order to pass off his weak thoughts, and it is an interesting question how long the world will be pleased to put up with such mediocre music."

Mendelssohn, on the contrary, in a letter comparing Liszt and Thalberg, who were the two great pianoforte rivals at that time, writes of "the heathen row" which Liszt created at Leipzig, and declares that Thalberg's calm way and self-control are much more worthy of the real *virtuoso.*

Undoubtedly Liszt's execution, the brilliance of which no one could deny, was apt at times to become too striking, literally as well as figuratively, for he was not infrequently known to send strings flying and hammers breaking. Chopin rather rubbed this in to him when he said to Liszt, "I prefer not to play in public; *you,* if you cannot charm the audience, can at least astonish and crush them." Mendelssohn pursues his comparison of Liszt and Thalberg with the remark that "Liszt's compositions rank beneath his execution, since above all he lacks ideas of his own, all his writing aiming only at showing off his virtuosity, whereas Thalberg's *Donna del Lago* — to instance one of his compositions—is a work of the most brilliant effect, with an astonishing gradual increase of difficulties and ornamentation, and showing refined taste in every bar: his power is as remarkable as is the light deftness of his fingers."

I will give you another great musician's comparison of the same two artists. Rubinstein at one of his historical recitals played Liszt's *Don Juan Fantasia,* and followed it immediately with Thalberg's on the same subject: when asked why he did so he said that "it was to show the difference between a god of music and a grocer." I need scarcely say which was which. My own recollection of Thalberg is of a tall, handsome, aristocratic man, who was invariably kindly and courteous: he sat quite immoveable at the piano, even when playing the most difficult passages: he had an exquisite touch and an unfailing technique, but, while one admired him immensely, one could never become enthusiastic over him.

One of the greatest merits of both his composition and his playing lay in his judicious use of the pedal. He wrote the greater part of his melodies for the middle of the piano, sustaining them by means of the pedal, while he adorned them both above and below with arpeggi, scales and arabesques, to such an extent as sometimes to give the effect of two performers when only one was playing. These ornamentations, which

were absolutely new at the time, quickly became the rage, and were done to death by his imitators.

Besides his own compositions, which he rendered to perfection, I heard him play *Bach,* when he gave one a perfect exposition of clear part playing, *Beethoven,* whom he always made dry and uninteresting, and *Schumann,* with whom he did not seem to have the slightest affinity. He *sang* his melodies on the piano, and his ornamentation was like beautiful lace-work, adorning a body externally beautiful, but possessing no soul; even when he played them himself his compositions were sadly lacking in this vital element.

Alfred Jaell was the Pugno of his day. He was a very short, tremendously stout little man, excellently groomed,

I will conclude this chapter with a brief *resume* of the musical career of Clara Schumann, the greatest female pianist the world has known. She made her first appearance in England in 1856, playing at the Philharmonic, Musical Union, and at her own recital at the Hanover Square Rooms. A dead set was made against her by the Press, headed by Davidson of the *Times,* and consequently she left England severely alone until 1865, when she met with considerable success. She returned again in 1867, and from then on she visited England nearly every year. The great success which she and other talented foreign artists were now achieving here, as compared with the cold reception hitherto accorded them, was due in a large measure to the great improvement in the public's taste and knowledge of music, which enabled audiences to fly in the face of a hostile press, and to form their own opinion as to what was worthy of their support. I had the pleasure of meeting Madame Schumann frequently, and used always to turn over for her at the Crystal Palace Concerts. When playing with orchestra she always used notes, not excepting the occasions when she played her husband's concerto. I was very proud when she asked me to play this concerto for her at a rehearsal, which she was unable to attend through indisposition. The many excellent portraits of Madame Schumann make it unnecessary for me to dwell upon her personal appearance. One thing, however, that always struck me was her look of absolute absorption in her work. I don't think I ever saw any artist more completely wrapped up in her art: she never thought of herself, but only of the composition she happened to be playing, her whole soul steeped in the work she was rendering.

In her playing there was never the smallest suspicion of self-display, never the smallest departure from the text. Every *nuance* marked by the composer was most conscientiously attended to. She was the classical *pianiste par excellence.*

Her hands might have been made for piano playing: they were broad, with thick soft-cushioned fingers, which were capable of a magnificent stretch, enabling her to play tenths with the utmost ease. She always held her fingers quite close to the key-board, so as to give the impression almost of kneading the keys: as a result one could never hear the click of the keys when she was playing, except perhaps in very brilliant passage work. Her octaves she played in the modern way, with loose wrist and by a fall of the hand, not a blow. One fault she had, which nearly all her contemporaries shared, and which was no doubt due to the thin tone of the pianos of the period, the fault of arpeggiing nearly all her chords. She was also a composer of distinct merit — a fact, I believe, not generally known. The influence of her husband's compositions is obvious throughout her works, which invariably show the hand of a thorough musician and frequently possess a distinctly graceful vein of melody.

CHAPTER IV. LEIPZIG IN THE 'SIXTIES. HE great educational musical centre in the 'sixties was Leipzig; and when, in 1864, I found myself free to devote some time to study, I naturally selected that town, and became a student at the Conservatoire there. This institute was founded by Mendelssohn in 1843 under the modest title of "Music School". The promoters were Mendelssohn, Schumann, Hauptmann, David, Pohlenz, and Becker. The staff of professors was joined by Moscheles in 1846 and by Reinecke in i860.

Moscheles was the principal professor of pianoforte playing in 1864, and I became a student in his class. I have nothing but pleasant recollections of my old master both in his teaching and private capacity. He was short of stature, with a distinctly Jewish cast of countenance: he had excellent pianoforte hands, broad and muscular, and trained to perfection in the old school of pianoforte playing. His finger technique was excellent, but he played everything with the rigid arm and wrist of the period; as a result of which his octaves were inclined to be heavy, and his playing was to a certain extent lacking in variety of tone. He was fond of rhythmical accentuation, and made a great point of strict adherence to time. For this reason he did not appreciate Chopin, and always refused to teach his compositions, on the ground that he "was unable to play out of time."

His favourite composers were Beethoven, Weber, Mendelssohn, and—Moscheles. Alas! his compositions are now almost forgotten, with the exception of his G minor Concerto and his Studies, Opus 70. The latter will, I think, live for a long while yet, as they are excellent preparatory studies for all composers up to and including Beethoven. His works showed a distinct advance on those of his great predecessor Hummel, his harmonies and modulations being more modern, and his melodies having greater depth.

As a man, apart from his teaching, Moscheles had a wonderful charm. I spent many a pleasant Sunday afternoon at his house, where he was fond of chatting to me about his English experiences. He had resided in England for twenty years, from 1826 to 1846, during which period he was conductor and director of the Philharmonic Society, and, I believe, he was also professor for some time at the Royal Academy of Music: he was certainly the most popular teacher of the pianoforte in London. His pupils included Mendelssohn, Thalberg, Litolff, Lindsay Sloper, O'Leary, Franklin Taylor, Dannreuther, Barnett, &c. Some of his experiences in England were distinctly funny. I remember one of them. He was engaged to give lessons to the two daughters of a certain noble lord. He went to the house and rang the visitors' bell; the footman who opened the door told him to ring the servants' bell, as the music-master was not allowed to go up the visitors' staircase. Moscheles naturally resented this and left the house. The noble lord apologised, and lessons were arranged; but when they came to an end Moscheles had the greatest difficulty in getting his fees, which were eventually paid in instalments. The social position of musicians does not seem to have been much better abroad in those days, judging by a testimonial which Moscheles received from Albrechtsberger, from whom he took lessons in counterpoint. He showed it to me with great glee. As far as my memory serves me, it ran somewhat like this: "I hereby certify that Ignaz Moscheles has studied most diligently with me for such and such a time, and that he has made such good progress that I consider him competent to gain an honest livelihood wherever he may chance to settle down"! This sounds more like a recommendation to a journeyman tailor or bootmaker than a testimonial to one of the finest musicians of his time. Moscheles was particularly proud of the fact that he had been selected by 'Mr.' Beethoven, as he always called him, to arrange the orchestral score of *Fidelio* for the pianoforte.

As a teacher he was most painstaking and patient, and I learnt a great deal from him with regard to correct accentuation and phrasing, but of touch and tone colour little or nothing. He was very particular about what he termed his staccato playing—all done with stiff arm and wrist He was explaining this one day to an American, who was in his class, and using his gold pencil-case to illustrate his point. "If this were a red-hot poker," he said, "you would not touch it so—but *so*—and that is my staccato." To which the Yankee coolly replied, "If that were a red-hot poker, Professor, I guess I wouldn't touch it at all." Moscheles joined in the laugh that greeted this answer as heartily as any of us students. One of his best pianoforte compositions was a piece called *Les Contrastes,* for two pianos and eight hands, which I had the pleasure of playing with him in public in Leipzig.

Of my other Professors the most eminent were Friedrich Richter (counterpoint), Carl Reinecke (pianoforte), and Ferdinand David *(ensemble* playing and conducting). To the last-named I am especially grateful for the great benefit I derived from his lessons. As I had had a great deal of experience in accompanying at the Crystal Palace, he always chose me to accompany his violin pupils. He had a most violent temper, and many a time have I seen the music thrown to the other end of the room and the culprit sent after it. But the storm soon blew over, and if a pupil were lucky enough to do anything well he got a corresponding amount of praise. I dearly loved his lessons. He, alas I has gone now, with all the rest, except Reinecke, whom I had the pleasure of seeing last year in Leipzig. I had a delightful chat with the old fellow, whom I found at his desk composing. He lives in a second-floor flat, but although he is nearly eightythree years old he told me the stairs did not bother him at all, as he was still very firm upon his feet. But, musically, I am afraid he has not gone with the times. In speaking of *Xh & Meistersinger* he admitted that it was the finest libretto that had ever been written for music, but expressed a regret that *he* had not had it, for "he would have written very different music to it. " I discreetly said "Jawohl, Herr Professor." Poor old fellow! his music would have been *very* different! Not that his compositions lack merit—they are all free from vulgarity and eminently graceful; one of the best of them is his Pianoforte Concerto in Fsharp, which I had the pleasure of playing under his conductorship at the Gewandhaus Concerts in 1871.

Finding out after a short time that the teaching of touch and technique was entirely ignored by the Professors at the Conservatoire, I looked around me to

see if I could find someone in Leipzig who would bemean himself by teaching this most essential branch of the art, and I eventually applied to Louis Plaidy, who had quarrelled with the authorities and had left the Conservatoire, to give me private lessons. Plaidy then had the reputation of being the best teacher in Europe of pianoforte technique. I had lessons from him for nearly two years, and found him quite the most brilliant master of touch and technique I had yet come across.

Plaidy was the first to publish a really good book of Technical Studies for the pianoforte, of which hundreds of thousands of copies have been sold all over the world. In this work he advocated transposing the exercises into different keys, retaining the C major fingering throughout, regardless of black keys: he thus had the distinction of initiating our modern fingering.

Another of the shining lights of Saxony at that period was Robert Franz, the greatest song writer after Schubert. I stayed with him several times in Halle, where he was conductor of the Symphony Concerts; and he played me many of his songs, a great many of them still in manuscript. I shall never forget the shock 1 received one day when I asked him why he left out the lower octaves in a piece he was playing. He told me that he was entirely deaf to the lower and higher notes of the piano, and that his hearing was gradually and progressively narrowing, until it would finally cease at the middle C. This most unfortunately proved to be the case, and he eventually became stone deaf. He was the world's greatest authority on Bach and Handel, and had arranged nearly all Bach's orchestral works for modern orchestra.

Apart from the excellent instruction to be obtained in Leipzig there was a wonderful musical atmosphere about the place, which made it far and away the best trainingground for the aspiring student, who, when there, was literally saturated with music. There were the Gewandhaus Concerts, to the final rehearsals of which we students were admitted free; the Euterpe Concerts,

where modern works were most in evidence; the Opera, an excellent one, to the stalls of which the students could go for ninepence; and though these had no backs to them, our musical ardour scorned the petty discomfort. In addition, we had our Musical Union, and our Debating Society for the discussion of the musical questions of the day. I had the *entree* to the house of Julius Kistner, the great music publisher, who, poor fellow, was partially paralyzed, and could not go about at all. I was very lucky to know him, as I met all the great artists of the period at his house, including Robert Franz, Joachim, Rubinstein, Marie Krebs, Asanchewski, Alfred Jaell, Dreyschock, Marchesi —in short, nearly all the stars of the musical firmament.

Amongst my fellow-students at Leipzig there were many who have since made their mark in the musical world. Nearly every nation was represented there: England by Cowen, Swinnerton Heap, and Stephen Adams; America by Perabo, Petersilia, and Hofmann; Germany by Wilhelmj, Kleinmichel, Frank, Heckmann, von Bernuth, Volkland, and Kogel; Scandinavia by Grieg and Johann Svendsen; and Hungary by Robert Freund and Joseffy— to take a few of the most prominent representatives of each country.

A favourite haunt of ours was a cafe called "Zum Kaffee-Baum," and I remember an old waiter there whom we used to draw out to tell us stories of Schumann, whose "Kneipe" it was, and whom this old fellow had always served. Amongst other things he told us that Schumann would drink his fifteen Seidel of beer in an evening without uttering a word, although surrounded by friends: he would sit in absolute silence, entirely absorbed, and occasionally rapping out a rhythm on the table with his fingers, as though he were evolving some new composition. This, he declared, would happen evening after evening.

Our great time for playing the fool was when the Leipzig Fair was on. This was really a very important affair, as it was the great book and music-mart for that part of the country, and people used to flock to it from great distances. We used to take a fiendish delight in changing the trade-signs on the different booths after the fair was closed at night, putting a baker's sign over a hosier's booth, a boot-maker's over a butcher's, and so on. We were caught red-handed one evening by the night-watchmen, and were ignominiously hauled off to the policestation, where, however, we were let off with a caution. We had our revenge a few nights later, when a number of us ostentatiously passed the watchmen with big strips of pasteboard tucked under our arms. When they saw us they fell into our trap, and thinking that we were at our sign-changing games again, gave us chase, and we led them a pretty dance as long as our wind held out. When at last we were caught, we were injured innocence personified, and indignantly asked if it was the custom in Leipzig to pursue and arrest people for carrying sketching-blocks under their arms!

These and other recollections came vividly back to my mind when I visited the dear old place last year. I found the town altered and enlarged almost out of recognition, and I hailed with joy the few old places that were still in existence, such as Auerbach's Keller, immortalized in *Faust,* and the famous old Gewandhaus in the Ritterstrasse.

In 1866 war broke out between Prussia and Austria. Belonging, as she did, to the South German Federation, Saxony was bound, though sorely against the grain, to side with Austria. I saw Leipzig taken by the Prussians without a shot being fired: indeed many of the Leipzig ladies threw bouquets to the soldiers as they entered to take possession of the town. Nevertheless, everything was at a complete standstill, so far as music was concerned: the Conservatoire was closed, and, as no one had the slightest idea that the war would be over so soon, Moscheles advised me to return to England, which advice I followed.

CHAPTER V. TAUSIG AS TEACHER AND "THE HIGHER DEVELOPMENT."
FTER a two years' stay in England I

went for a further period of study to Berlin, where Tausig, who was then at the zenith of his fame, had recently opened his "School for the Higher Development of Pianoforte Playing." When I applied for admission to his classes, Ehlert, who was his second-in-command, accompanied me on my first visit to the great man, and on the way gave me some points as to Tausig's ways and disposition. I found him, as Ehlert had foretold, a nervous, over-wrought man, who was charming if he liked one, but very much the reverse if he did not. To anyone who was not in sympathy with him he was capable of being fiendishly sarcastic; his condemnation of those whom he disliked totally lacked the element of charity.

On that occasion his greeting was the reverse of genial. With a shrug of his shoulders, he said, "Oh! you come from England? Well, play something." I went to the big Concert Grand and began with a crashing chord—and, lo and behold! a soft, muffled sound came from the instrument, instead of the crash I expected. I looked up and saw Tausig watching me with a sardonic smile. I lost my temper and went on headlong with my playing, too angry at the moment to care for Tausig or anybody else. After a while he stopped me; and, a trifle more graciously, said, "Yes, I will take you—come to my class to-morrow. " I found out later that Tausig hated his practising being heard, and so had had the hammers of his piano felted so heavily as almost to kill all sound.

How shall I describe Tausig to you? His character varied so with his mood that a consistent description is almost impossible. In personal appearance he was a very small, slightly-built man with very piercing, dark eyes, and hair already turning grey, although he was only 27 years old. He practised nearly all day long, except the four hours on two days in the week which he devoted to teaching. His only recreations were the reading of metaphysical works—particularly Kant, Hegel, and Schoppenhauer—and chess, of which game he was one of the best exponents in Berlin at that time.

As a teacher he was most minutely particular: a wrong note to him was like a red rag to a bull, while if your phrasing was wrong you were overwhelmed by a torrent of stinging sarcasm. I recollect two instances: I was playing Henselt's study, *Si oisean f'etais,* not as Henselt wrote it, but with three notes in each hand, and staccato, which made it almost impossibly difficult to play for anyone but Tausig himself. When I had played a few bars he swept me off the stool with the remark, "My dear Beringer, those are English birds—they can't fly, they have lime on their wings. " Then he played it—Heavens I how he played it—prestissimo, yet with every note as clear as crystal. On another occasion a Russian Countess was playing rather heavily: he raged about the room for some time, and at last stopped at the piano and said, "You play like a rhinoceros." She very quietly retorted, "You really must not call me such names." He said, "Oh, commence again." After another perambulation of the room, he stopped her once more at the same bar, and said, "My dear Countess, what can I do? You *do* play just like a rhinoceros. "

Although in Berlin, owing to its much greater size, the musical life was nothing like so concentrated as in Leipzig, the student there had constant opportunities of hearing first-class music. What with the Opera, the Philharmonic Concerts, Bilse's Orchestral Concerts, Joachim's Quartette, and the frequent performances of light and Italian opera at Kroll's Garten, not to speak of recitals without number, the most voracious musical appetite was bound to get its fill.

The Opera House witnessed some exciting scenes in those days, as the Wagner controversy was then at its height, and although the great composer had already won many staunch supporters to his side, much of the hostility with which his first efforts were received was still displayed at the production of every fresh work. I shall never forget the first performance of *Die Meistersinger,* which was produced shortly after the publication by Wagner of a pamphlet upon the pernicious influence of Judaism on music, in which Meyerbeer and Mendelssohn came in for special censure. The rich Berlin Jews determined to have their revenge, and, having bought up the whole of the dearer parts of the house, sent in their employes armed with rattles, dog-whistles, and a thousand-and-one noise-creating instruments. The first bar of the overture was the signal for the letting loose of Pandemonium—rattles were sprung, whistles blown, horns sounded, and the din was added to by the shouts and cries of the Wagnerites (most of us were in the gallery) striving to drown noise by noise, and only succeeding in adding to the uproar. It was quite the most exciting musical, or rather ««musical, evening I have ever spent. Niemann, the great tenor, was cast for the part of *Walther,* and as he was immensely popular, his *Pteisslied* was listened to, but this was the only number I heard that night. However, the opera was proceeded with to the bitter end, and, in spite of all opposition, *Die Meistersinger* won on its merits, and was more frequently performed during the season than any other opera.

1 had the good fortune during my stay in Berlin to meet a number of well-known musicians, amongst the most noteworthy being Adolph Henselt, Franz Bendel, Adolph Jensen, and Marie Krebs, and my intercourse with these and many other shining lights of the musical world has left behind it none but pleasant memories.

When war broke out between France and Germany musical life in Berlin was more or less at a standstill, and when Tausig gave up his school, towards the end of 1870, I returned once more to England. Since that date my work, with the exception of some concert-playing at Leipzig and elsewhere in Germany, has been entirely confined to this country. Fresh from Tausig's influence, my great ambition was to open an institution in London upon the lines of his school at Berlin. I received very cordial support for my project, and in 1871 the School for the Higher Development of Pianoforte-playing was opened in London, under the presidency of Franklin Taylor, with Walter Bache, Fritz Hartvigson, Ebenezer Prout, myself, and others, as professors. For some reason or other the title, "For the Higher Development &c." which was in imitation of that of Tausig's school, drew down the vials of wrath upon our devoted heads from all the musical critics of the period. They went for us for all they were worth, and chaffed us unmercifully. In this case, however, ridicule did *not* kill—in fact their attack did us nothing but good. They were particularly generous in coupling the title of our school with the playing of Rubinstein and Biilow for mutual criticism and condemnation. In this they were "cruel only to be kind," as we got, free gratis and for nothing, the finest advertisement we could possibly have wished for, and, in consequence, our numbers went up by leaps and bounds.

I should like to read you a quotation from the *Daily Telegraph* and one from the *Musical World* by Davidson of the *Times.* The *Telegraph* article ran as follows:—

"Herr v. Biilow is the champion of a new school of pianoforte-playing represented among us by an institution for the 'higher development' of this branch of executive art.

'"Higher development' is a vague term. It sounds well, we admit, and like the old Scotchwoman's comforting 'Mesopotamia' can be 'rolled, a sweet morsel, under the tongue.' But experience of Herr v. Biilow's playing suggests a rather anxious inquiry into the particulars of this 'higher development.' What does it mean? Professors of 'higher development' have not as a rule proved themselves remarkable for perfect execution—Herr v. Biilow, for example, sometimes drops his notes, or sometimes plays *wrong* notes, but the ecstacies of 'higher development' theorists are not at all abated in consequence. We are bound therefore to search out their distinctive principles without reference to a strictly accurate rendering of the text. Does the new school take the bodily action of the performer under its care? Judging from observation, we should expect to find in the curriculum a course of exercises giving special heed to that style of 'going' which belongs to high-stepping horses, and laying down rules as to when an audience may be contemplated with best effect, and when it is most advisable that the raptured eyes should be elevated to the ceiling.

"Herr v. Biilow, the incarnation of higher development, ministers to that craving for sensation which is the curse of modern music. He plays without the book, and the public act as if an astounding memory demonstrated astounding artistic capacity. His playing, while often remarkable in the true sense, is more often noteworthy for an impulsiveness so headlong that trips and stumbles are the result. Lastly, he treats the compositions of the greatest masters with a daring which in itself has a certain fascination. We watch Blondin on the high rope with an interest, which is none the less great because it is painful, and in like manner we cannot but watch Herr v. Biilow deal with a Beethoven concerto or sonata. While fully acknowledging his command over an audience, and admiring the energy and ability which accompany it, we must hold that the artistic influence of Herr v. Biilow is far from an unmixed good."

Davidson, in the *Musical World,* attacked Rubinstein through the mouths of two fictitious people, "Baylis Boyle" and "Purple Powis," to this effect:—

"BOYLE (loudly): Was that thunder?

"POWIS (softly): No, it was Rubinstein.

"BOYLE: The impression produced by his playing was such as virtually to impose silence upon his fellow pianists. I could not hear Barth, nor Halle, nor Krebs, nor Mehlig, nor Zimmerman, nor Dannreuther, nor Beringer, nor Hartvigson, nor Coenen, nor Franklin Taylor, nor Billy Holmes, nor Lindsay Sloper, nor even Brekner.

"POWIS: Oh, yes, I heard Breitner.

"BOYLE: Donner und Blitzen.

"POWIS: I will telegraph von Biilow and—

"BOYLE (suddenly): No, Franz Liszt

is coming. He will 'sous terre' them all.

"POWIS: Aye, and impose silence."

And then followed a caricature of Rubinstein (reproduced on the opposite page) under fche heading "Highest Development."

But though this was the general attitude of the Press at that time towards these two great artists, there was already growing up in England a musical public which was beginning to have an opinion "of its own on matters musical and to fly in the face of bigoted newspaper criticism. To them it was obvious that von Biilow and Rubinstein were the greatest pianists of their day after Liszt and Tausig, and the fact that our School for the Higher Development was involved in this unwarrantably bitter attack served only to recommend it. The school flourished exceedingly, and it was not until 1898, when, under pressure of my steadily-increasing work as a professor at the Royal Academy of Music and an examiner for the Associated Board of the Royal Academy and Royal College of Music, I was faced with the necessity of either closing my school or severing my connection with those institutions, that I chose the former alternative.

CHAPTER VI. FOUR GIANTS OF THE PIANOFORTE. IF the latter half of the nineteenth century had given us no pianoforte players of note besides the four who form the subject of the present chapter—Liszt, Tausig, von Biilow and Rubinstein—it would still have stood out as a period of singular richness, a seven fat years of talent. With four such giants as these, what would it have mattered had the rest been pygmies?

To *Franz Liszt,* who towers high above all his predecessors, must be given pride of place.

In 1870 I had the good fortune to go with Tausig to the Beethoven Festival held at Weimar by the Allgemeiner Musik Verein, and there I met Liszt for the first time. I had the opportunity of learning to know him from every point of view, as Pianist, Conductor, Composer, and, in his private capacity, as a *man*—and every aspect seemed to me equally magnificent.

His remarkable personality had an indescribable fascination, which made itself felt at once by all who came into contact with him. This wonderful magnetism and power to charm all sorts and conditions of men was illustrated in a delightful way. He was walking down Regent Street one day, on his way to his concert at the St. James' Hall. As he passed the cab-rank, he was recognised, and the cabbies as one man took off their hats and gave three rousing cheers for "The Habby Liszt." The man who can evoke the enthusiasm of a London cabby, except by paying him treble his fare, is indeed unique and inimitable!

As a *Conductor,* the musical world owes him an undying debt of gratitude for having been the first to produce Wagner's *Lohengrin,* and to revive *Tannhduser* in the face of the opprobrium heaped upon this work by the whole of the European press. It was he, too, who first produced Berlioz's *Benvenuto Cellini* and many other works, which, though neglected and improperly understood at that time, have since come into their kingdom and received due recognition.

As a *Composer* I do not think that Liszt has hitherto been esteemed as highly as he deserves. If only for having invented the "Symphonic Poem," which was an absolutely new form of orchestral composition, he has merited the highest honours; while his pre-eminence is still undisputed in the *bravura* style of pianoforte works, without one or more of which no pianoforte recital seems complete. The same compliment is not paid his orchestral works, which are performed far too rarely.

Words cannot describe him as a *Pianist*—he was incomparable and unapproachable. I have seen whole rows of his audience, men and women alike, affected to tears, when he chose to be pathetic: in stormy passages he was able by his art to work them up to the highest pitch of excitement: through the medium of his instrument he played upon every human emotion. Rubinstein, Tausig and Biilow all admitted that they were mere children in comparison with Liszt. Wagner said of his playing of Beethoven's Sonatas Opus 106 and Opus m that "those who never heard him play them in a friendly circle could not know their real meaning. His was not a *re-production*—it was a *re-creation." Tausig,* to whom in his capacity as a teacher I have referred in the preceding chapter, merits the second place in this quartette of honour. As far as technique was concerned he stood head and shoulders above everyone else.

Weitzmann says of him, "Tausig is the Mephistopheles of pianoforte *virtuosi.* With a power that is little short of demoniacal, he can in turn freeze the blood in one's veins, as he performs the most amazingly daring feats of virtuosity, and again, by his stormy outbursts of uncontrolled passion, send it coursing along like molten fire. The strength and unfailing quality of his performances borders on the incredible."

Billow, on the last occasion when he heard Tausig play, said to him, "You have become unapproachably great, my dear friend. Unfailing as my admiration of your gigantic talent has always been, I never believed it possible that I should one day esteem you as highly as I did Joachim, when I heard him play the Beethoven Concerto. Every note you play is golden, the quintessence of musical feeling." He went on to tell Tausig the story of Horace Vernet, who on one occasion drew a wonderfully clever little sketch in a friend's album in the short space of ten minutes. His friend expressed surprise at Vernet's celerity of execution. "What!" retorted Vernet, "You think I have only expended ten minutes on your album? I tell you I have put a good solid thirty years' work into it." "Thus of your playing, my dear Tausig," continued Biilow, "one may say, that in one short Prelude or Mazurka of Chopin is embraced the entire history of the art of pianoforte-playing from its earliest beginnings down to the present day."

Last, but certainly not least, the great Liszt said of Tausig, "Briareus himself, had it occurred to him to play the piano, could never, with all his hundred hands, have equalled this Tausig of the ten brazen fingers."

Again, referring to the untimely death of Tausig in 1871, at the early age of thirty-one, Liszt pathetically remarked to me (this was in London, in 1886), that he "wondered why it should have pleased God to take away our dear little Tausig, when there were so many fools left on this earth, who could so easily have been spared."

There can be little doubt that Tausig, had he lived, would have won further laurels for himself as a composer: as it was, he had written a pianoforte Concerto, Symphonic Poems, and many orchestral works of great promise. Some of these were published, but, becoming dissatisfied with them, he bought up all the copies and burnt them, starting afresh, a few years before his death, with his Studies as Opus I. In his arrangement of Strauss' Waltzes and *The Invitation to Dance* of Weber, he initiated an entirely novel form of pianoforte technique the embellishments and arabesques which he introduced into these works were at the time quite original, though they have since found one imitator in Godowsky. *Von Billow* first came to England in 1873, and I had the good fortune to become acquainted with him soon after his arrival, and he remained my friend until his death. I saw a great deal of him in 1884, when he generally spent two or three evenings a week at my house; and, in spite of his unruly tongue, which was frequently bitterly sarcastic, I learnt to love him, and to marvel more and more at the profound knowledge he possessed, not only of musical subjects, but of almost every topic under the sun.

He frequently used to stay until two or three in the morning, but the hours flew by like minutes, and it was not until his departure that one realised how long one had been talking. His was the most phenomenal memory I ever came across. On one evening he played nearly the whole of Brahms' pianoforte works by heart: on another, a number of the less known compositions of Liszt: and on a third occasion, when we were discussing the improvements made in orchestration, he showed that he had nearly every score of importance literally at his fingers' ends. I had the honour of playing Brahms' Grand Duet on a Chorale of Haydn for two pianos with Bilow at his last recital in 1888.

What can I say of him from a purely pianistic point of view? He played everything of real merit and played them all brilliantly, but I think he was greatest in the three "B's", as he called them—Bach, Beethoven, and Brahms.

But it was not only as a pianist that Biilow won the highest honours; he was also one of the greatest conductors of the last century. He brought his Meiningen Orchestra to such a pitch of perfection that he was able to play upon it almost as if it were an instrument under his hands. He made long tours through many parts of Europe with Brahms, with whom he interchanged roles, so that, while on one evening Brahms would play and Biilow conduct, the next saw Biilow playing, Brahms conducting. These tours were phenomenally successful.

As an editor, too, he deserves great praise: every student of pianoforte music owes Biilow a debt of gratitude for his edition of the later Sonatas of Beethoven, of the Chromatic Fantaisie of Bach, and of many other important works.

No reference to Biilow would be complete without some allusion to the trenchant wit for which he was so noted. I will quote one or two characteristic instances. The first was at my own expense. In 1885 I was giving a Bach Concert in celebration of the 200th anniversary of his birth, and my programme included the D minor Concerto for one piano, the C minor for two, the C major for three, and the A major for four pianos. Bulow was tickled at the notion, and said, "Very clever idea, Beringer, but rather like a circus, isn't it? You know, first on one horse, then on two, then on three, and then on four."

He made another amusing remark, during a lesson which he was giving a young lady on Beethoven's Sonata *VAdieu, LAbsence, et Le Retour.* In the introduction to the last movement (The Return) a stormy passage occurs, and Bulow told her that to realise the spirit of this, she must imagine that she had seen the prodigal in the distance and was rushing down the stairs to meet him, waving her handkerchief. Unfortunately the pupil broke down in the passage, and Bulow snapped out, "There 1 now you've trod on your skirt, fallen on your nose, and made an utter fiasco of the meeting."

Again, just before one of his recitals he told me that he wanted to play something of Bennett's, and had selected "The Parlourmaid" Sonata. It was some time before my dull brain grasped what he was getting at—Bennett's "Maid of Orleans" Sonata!

It is not generally known, I believe, that Bulow also composed works which show a considerable amount of talent. One of his best pianoforte works is *The Carnival of Milan,* which deserves to be better known, if only for the sake of its sparkling Intermezzo.

We now come to the last of these four giants of the piano:—*Rubinstein.* Though I met him on many occasions, I never came into such close personal relations with him as I did with Bulow.

Rubinstein, who was born in Russia, but of Jewish parents, in his playing showed much more of the Tartar than of the Jew. His methods were absolutely opposed to those of Biilow, whose playing was always intellectually thought out and technically filed down with the most minute care, while Rubinstein used to leave everything to the impulse of the moment; and, in consequence, was extraordinarily unequal. At one time he played like a god; at another, when he let his passions run away with him, like a barbarian. Those, however, who heard him play such pieces as Mozart's Rondo in A minor, or the F minor Variations of Haydn, are never likely to forget the wonderful tenderness and indescribable charm with which this Storm-Compeller was able to invest them,, for all the world like a Nasmyth steam-hammer, which, though capable of a blow of many hundred tons, can yet be made to break the glass of a watch, without damaging the works in the slightest degree.

He afforded wonderful proof of the

many-sidedness of his powers, when, in 1887, he gave his memorable series of seven historical recitals in London. At these he played specimens of all the composers of note, from Bull and Purcell, two of the earliest writers of Spinet and Clavichord music, up to and including those of his own period. The pieces he selected included most of the compositions that possess real merit; so that this, besides being a great artistic achievement, was, in addition, a prodigious feat of memory.

Although he was a composer of no mean ability, he was far too prolific, and sadly wanting in self-criticism. As a result, the value of his compositions varies considerably: some of his works reach a very high standard, their melodies showing genuine feeling and depth, while others are dry-as-dust and uninteresting, and contain far too much obvious padding.

CHAPTER VIL TOUCH.
'"THE wonderful improvement in pianoforte-playing made during the last fifty years is to a great extent attributable to the steady development during that period of the modern ideas and theories concerning *Touch.*

Touch, which nowadays we rightly regard as of vital importance, was almost entirely neglected fifty years ago. The present physiological treatment of this most important subject was undreamt-of at that time—no real theory of Touch existed. Where a player *did* use the right methods, it was by the light of nature solely that he did so; his instinct brought him to the same conclusions that we have arrived at by the light of reason. Such players as this were, however, few and far between; the old stiff- « arm and wrist tradition was still subscribed to by the majority of players, including artists of the first rank such as Moscheles, Kalkbrenner, Cramer and Clementi.

To Plaidy and Thalberg the credit is due of having been the first to break loose from this tradition.
Plaidy first taught octave-playing by a fall with the weight of the hand from a loose wrist and supported arm, which excellent practice has been from time

to time exaggerated to such an extent, that pupils often were, and in a few cases still are, taught to throw their hands as far back from the wrists as possible, and to strike the keys with the full force of the blow—a most pernicious habit. Another rule which he insisted upon was that in the position of the hand for finger exercises the centre of gravity should lean towards the thumb, and not, as hitherto taught, towards the little finger. In melodious playing he held that the fingers should be kept on the surface of the keys, and pressed firmly down upon them, this pressure being maintained until the next key was depressed. Curiously, he did not realize that this unnecessary continuance of pressure, after the production of the tone required, was a total waste of force. *Thalberg* laid still greater stress upon the touch question in regard to cantabile playing. In the preface to his work, "The Art of Singing applied to the Pianoforte" he says:—
"The art of singing well, a celebrated woman once said, is the same, to whatever instrument it be applied. And such is the fact. No concession or sacrifice should be made to the particular mechanism of any instrument; it is the task of the executant to subject that mechanism to the will of his art. As the piano cannot, *rationally* speaking, reproduce the highest quality of singing—namely the faculty of prolonging sounds—we must, by dint of skilfulness and art, overcome this defect, and succeed not only in producing the illusion of *sustained* and *prolonged* notes, but also of *swelling* notes.
"One of the first conditions for obtaining breadth of execution as well as pleasing sonority and great variety in the production of sound, is to lay aside all stiffness. It is therefore indispensable for the player to possess as much suppleness and as many inflexions in the fore-arm, the wrist, and the fingers, as a skilful singer possesses in his voice.
"In broad, noble, and dramatic songs, we must *sing from the chest.* Similarly we must require a great deal from the piano, and draw from it all the sound it can emit, not by *striking* the keys, but by playing on them from a very short

distance; by *pushing them down,* by *pressing* them with vigour, energy, and warmth. In simple, sweet, and graceful melodies, we must, so to speak, *knead* the piano; *tread* it with a hand without bones, and fingers of velvet: in this case the keys ought to be *felt* rather than *struck.*

"There is one thing which I must not omit to recommend, and that is, that the player should observe great moderation in the movements of his body, and great repose of the arms and hands; that he should never hold his hands too high above the keyboard; that he should always listen to himself when playing; that he should subject himself to severe self-criticism, and learn to judge his own performance. As a rule, players work too much with their fingers and too little with their intelligence."

This extract, copied from a work written close upon fifty years ago, shows how advanced were Thalberg's ideas upon this most essential feature of pianoforte-playing.
Dr. Adolph Kullak, in his 'Esthetic of Pianoforteplaying", published in 1876, was the first to speak of "the fall of the finger," which phrase inevitably implies that the weight comes from the hand or arm: for otherwise, the uncontrolled fall of the fingers would not be heavy enough to produce a tone. Kullak further insists upon looseness of wrist, and finger-pressure in cantabile playing.
Germer, in his book on Tone-Production, holds to the old system of finger-work, or rather *over-work,* but, with it, he advocates a loose arm.
To *Deppe* is due great credit for being the first to go in systematically for the loosely-supported arm in tone-production, but he was not sufficiently far advanced to realise the proper use of arm-weight in playing. CHAPTER VIII.
Caland, a pupil of Deppe, went further than her master. She fully recognised the necessity of using the upper arm, shoulder, and back. I will quote a few sentences from her book, which is called "Artistic Piano-playing."
"The hand must first of all be emancipated—must be quite free from the hampering weight of the arm. The hand

must be light as a feather. The hand will be light only when it is carried, instead of carrying itself over the keyboard. The lightness and freedom thus imparted to the hand is effected through the agency of the shoulder and arm muscles."

In 1881, *Du Bois Raymond,* in the epoch-making lectures he gave in Berlin upon the physiology of the muscles, and their relation to the movements of the body, gave a fresh and well-directed impulse to this quest for the best means, scientifically, of tone-production.

Since that date book after book has appeared on the subject. Their authors include *Marie Jaell,* many of whose conclusions are, to my mind, quite erroneous; *Sochting,* whose system is an amplification of Deppe's; and a host of others.

The soundness of *Leschetizky* upon the touch question, although he himself has not written any book upon the subject, is exemplified, not only by the admirable playing of his pupils, whose touch and tone-production are unexceptionable, but also by the writings of two of his disciples, *Marie Unschuld,* and *Malvine Bree,* who, in her book on the Leschetizky method, has a chapter on Cantabile playing, in which she strongly urges that the weight should be released, and the pressure on the key relaxed, immediately after tone-production: a point upon which Leschetizky himself laid stress,

Two important works by English authors have recently seen the light: they are, *TownsencCs* "Balance of Arm in Piano-Technique," published in 1903, and "The Act of Touch," by *Tobias Matthay.*

I now come to the two latest books upon the subject, both of them German publications: *Breithaupts* "Die Naturliche Klaviertechnik", in which he summarises, from the musician's point of view, all that has been said hitherto with regard to touch: and "The Physiological Mistakes in Pianoforte-playing, and How to Correct Them", by *Dr. Steinhausen,* an eminent German surgeon. This latter is, in my opinion, by far the most important work upon technique, from the physiological point of

view, that has appeared up to the present date.

The gist of these successive efforts to systematise and elevate touch and tone-production, seems to me to be contained in the following five rules:— 1. Avoid all stiffness in the joints, fingers, wrists, elbows, and shoulders. 2. Avoid the over-practice of any one particular movement, especially those affecting the weak fingermuscles. (It was the neglect of this precaution that led to the injuring, and in some cases, the permanent laming of the hand, which was so prevalent among pianists a few years ago.) 3. Discontinue pressure immediately after tone-production; continued pressure means unnecessary fatigue. 4. Use the whole weight of the arm for big toneproduction. 5. Make use of a rolling motion of the elbow for throwing weight from one side of the hand to the other, or even from finger to finger. CONCERTS AND PROGRAMMES. /"NE of the simplest methods of showing the enormous improvement in the musical taste of the English public will be to make a brief chronological survey of the concert programmes of the last fifty years.

The principal Concerts in the later 'fifties were the Musical Union Chamber Concerts (the forerunners of the Monday 'Pops'), the Philharmonic Concerts, the daily Concerts at the Crystal Palace, and Jullien's Promenade Concerts at the Surrey Gardens and Lyceum Theatre. At the Philharmonic the programme consisted chiefly of compositions of Haydn, Mozart, Beethoven, Weber, Mendelssohn, Spohr, Cherubini, Bennett, Hummel, Dussek, and Wolfel.

At the Crystal Palace the programme was of a much lighter description — one or two movements out of a Haydn or Mozart Symphony mixed up with operatic selections, waltzes by Strauss, cornet solos, etc. The Saturday Concerts were first started in i860, and from then on Sir August Manns, the conductor at the Palace, gradually educated his audiences, until, as we all know, his programmes became models of all that programmes should be, including all the

great classical works as well as everything new of any worth. To him are due the thanks of all English musicians for the encouragement he gave to contemporary English composers. I have no hesitation in saying that no man has done more for English music than August Manns. CHAPTER IX.

But when I tell you that in 1861 I played the Fantaisie de Concert on airs from *Maria,* by Kuhe, at one of these concerts, and that this was singled out by the Press for special praise as being the best item on the programme, you can imagine how carefully and how gradually Manns had to go to work, until at last his concerts reached that high standard of excellence which they maintained for so many years afterwards.

Excellent music was also to be heard at the Quartette Concerts, which owed their origin to a small but earnest band of musicians, amongst whom were Sterndale Bennett, Sainton, Piatti, and Charles Hall£, under whose aegis Arabella Goddard made her d£but. They did not, however, receive adequate support from the public, and were obliged to discontinue the concerts after three years.

Of course there was always a select circle of real music-lovers in London, who could appreciate good music, but it was a surprisingly small one. However, the public taste has improved since then to a marvellous degree, so that now one can find an audience of thousands, at the Promenade and Sunday concerts, listening to Beethoven, Wagner, etc. This improvement, to my mind, has been particularly pronounced in the last decade, so much so that such remarks as a certain lady made some years ago, on being asked whether she had been to the last Richter concert, are hardly likely ever to be heard again, at any rate amongst decently educated folks. "Oh dear no," she said, "I couldn't get a ticket for less than *10s. 6d.,* and I'm certainly not going to pay more than 5 J. to hear a *band* play!"

The Crystal Palace concerts have, in my opinion, done more than any others to foster a love of good music in the general public, and I will therefore give their programmes pride of place, starting with one that took place in 1859, I have unfortunately been unable to trace any of earlier date. Anyone comparing these programmes must at once be struck with the enormous difference in intrinsic musical value between the first one, of 1859, and the last, of 1890.

In referring to these concerts I should like to draw attention to the frequency with which the names of English composers appeared on the programmes. From the very first Manns gave them a cordial welcome, and his readiness to recognise unknown talent helped to set many of the youthful composers of this country on the first rung of the ladder of fame. On Arthur Sullivan's return from Leipzig, his first appearance was at the Palace in 1862, when he conducted his *The Tempest* music. This created quite a furore, and he was acclaimed by Press and public alike as the coming English composer *par excellence*. One of his works, a selection from *The Sapphire Necklace,* will be found in the second of the programmes I have selected, while the first contains an overture by Bennett Gilbert, another English composer of merit:— CRYSTAL PALACE.

Saturday Concert, September 17th, 1859.
PROGRAMME.
PART I.
SYMPHONY in B flat----*Haydn*. 1. Adagio and Allegro. 3. Minuetto Allegro. 2. Adagio. 4. Finale, Allegro Vivace.
GRAND ARIA from "Faust"---*Spohr*.
Madame Rudersdorff.
GLEE, "Discord, dire Sister"---*Webbe*.
Orpheus Glee Union.
SOLO for Flute *Boehm*. Mr. Alfred Wells.
SONG, "The Skylark"-*Foster*.
Madame Rudersdorff.
CONCERT OVERTURE in E flat--*Bennett Gilbert*. (First time of Performance.)
PART n. OVERTURE and ORGIE (The Huguenots) *Meyerbeer*.
IRISH MELODY, "The LastRose of Summer"
arranged by *T. Distin*. Orpheus Glee Union.
SOLO for Cornet, Canzonetta from "Di-

norah" *Meyerbeer*.
(Expressly arranged for M. Duhem by A. Manns.)
Cornet, Mr. Duhem.
SPANISH SONG. "La Calesero"--*Yradier*.
Madame Rudersdorff.
GLEE, "The Hunt is up"---*Hatton*.
Orpheus Glee Union.
FACKEL-TANZ-*Duke of CoburgGotha*.
(First time of Performance.)
Conductor, A. MANNS.

Saturday Concert, April 13th, 1867.
PROGRAMME.
OVERTURE, "Jessonda"-*Spohr*.
ARIA. "Non piu andrai"----*Mozart*.
Mons. De Fontanier.
RECITATIVE and ARIA, "Non temer amato bene"------*Mozart*.
Mdlle. Enquist. Violin Obbligato—Herr Straus. SYMPHONY No. 6. in F, "Pastorale"-*Beethoven*. SELECTION from the MS. Opera, "The
Sapphire Necklace"----*A.S.Sullivan*.
a. Introduction (Orchestra) — Sunset.
b. Recitative and Prayer, "Angels, who on high". c. Song, "Love will be master".
Miss Edith Wynne.
SOLO for Violin, Adagio and Rondo, from
Concerto in F sharp minor (No. 2)-*Vieuxtetnps*.
Herr Straus.
SONGS—a. "Lieblingsplatzchen"--*Mendelssohn*. b. "Gretchen am Spinnrade"-*Schubert*.
Mdlle. Enquist.
SONG, "A Presentiment"----*Ch. Luders*.
Mods. De Fontanier.
SONG, "Ave Maria"-*Schubert*.
Miss Edith Wynne.
OVERTURE to Byron's "Manfred"--*R. Schumann*.
A. MANNS, Conductor.
Saturday Concert, January 29th, 1876.
PROGRAMME. OVERTURE, "Fingal's Cave"-
SCENA and ARIA, "E dunque ver?" (First time at these Concerts.)
Miss Sophie L6we.
CONCERTO for Pianoforte and Orchestra, No. 3, in Gmajor (Op. 45) (First time at these Concerts.)
Mr. Oscar Beringer.

AIR, "Revenge, Timotheus cries" (Alexander's Feast)-----
Signor Foli.
SYMPHONY in D, (No. 2 of Salomon set) (First time at these Concerts.) LIED, "Du bist die Ruh"
SONG, "Hark, the lark"-
Miss Sophie Lowe.
RECITATIVE and ARIA, "Fu dio che disse"
Signor Foli. OVERTURE, "Les francs Juges"
A. MANNS, *Mendelssohn*.
Rubinstein.
-*Rubinstein. Handel*.
Haydn.
Schubert.
Apolloni. Berlioz.
Conductor.
Saturday Concert, 1885.
PROGRAMME.
OVERTURE. "Ariadne"----*Handel*.
(First time of performance here.) CHORUS, "Love and Hymen" (Hercules)-*Handel*.
The Crystal Palace Choir.
SYMPHONY in A major, "Italian"--*Mendelssohn*.
THE NOCTURNE-DUET from "Beatrice et Benedict" *Berlioz*.
Miss Annie Marriott and Miss Edith Marriott.
CONCERTO for Pianoforte and Orchestra in
C minor (Op. 185)----*Raff*.
Pianoforte—Mr. Oscar Beringer.
SONG, "The Wanderer"----*Schubert*.
Mr. Watkin Mills.
AIR and CHORUS, "Haste thee, nymph"-*Handel*.
Mr. Charles Chilley and Crystal Palace Choir.
THE CHORAL FANTASIA (Op. 80)--*Beethoven*.
Pianoforte—Mr. Oscar Beringer.
Miss Annie Marriott, Miss Edith Marriott,
Miss Annie Layton, Mr. Charles Chilley, Mr. Hirwin Jones,
Mr. Watkin Mills, and The Crystal Palace Choir.
BALLET AIRS from "Etienne Marcel"-*Saint-Saens*. (First time.)
A. MANNS, Conductor.
Saturday Concert, November 1st,

1890.

PROGRAMME OVERTURE, "Anacreon"----Cherubini. BENEDICTUS for Violins and Orchestra -A.C.Mackenzie. CONCERTO for Pianoforte and Orchestra-Schumann. Mons. Paderewski. AIR, "Come, Margarita, come" (The Martyr of Antioch) A. Sullivan. Mr. Ben Davies.

SYMPHONY, No. 3 in F (Op. 90)--Brahms.

SOLOS for Pianoforte:— a. Melody (Op. 16)---Paderewski. b. Rhapsody No. 12--Liszt. SERENADE, "Awake 1 Awake!"--Piatti. INVITATION to the Waltz (for Orchestra by

Berlioz)-----Weber.

Next in importance from an educational point of view were the Monday Popular Chamber Concerts, familiarly known as the Monday 'Pops'. They were started on Monday, January 3rd, 1859, and lasted without interruption until 1900.

From their first inception Joseph Joachim was connected with them, and their success was in a great measure due to the fact that this incomparable violinist figured so prominently on their programmes. If my memory does not play me false, he was the first to introduce Brahms' Chamber Music into England at one of these concerts.

Alfredo Piatti, whose 'cello playing was of almost equal excellence, was also associated with them from the beginning, and had a great share in their success. At one Of the Monday 'Pops' in 1884 I had the honour of playing with him and with Joachim in Dvorak's Trio, Op. 65.

Louis Ries, another of the performers there, was an excellent second violinist, while the viola was played by Doyle, Zerbini, Straus, Gibson, and others.

The two first programmes of this series will, I think, be found of especial interest, the music of the first being exclusively Italian, of the second exclusively English:— MONDAY POPULAR CONCERTS

AT THE ST. JAMES'S HALL.

Monday, February 27th, 1860.

PROGRAMME

(exclusively selected from the Vocal and Instrumental works of Italian Masters).

PART L

QUINTET, in E major (No. 6, third set, Op. 20), for 2 Violins, Viola, and Two Violoncellos Boccherini. (First time.)

Herr Becker, Herr Ries, Mr. Doyle, M. Paque, and Signor Piatti. ARIA, "Resta in pace, idolo mio" (Gl' Orazi ed i Curiazi)-Cimarosa. (First time.) Miss Susanna Cole.

REC1TATIVO e RONDO, "Ah non sai qual pena"-------Sarti. (First time.) Mdlle. Euphrosyne Parepa.

SCENA TRAGICA-GRAND SONATA, in

G minor, for Pianoforte alone (Di-done

Abbandonata)-----Clementi. (First time.)

Miss Arabella Goddard.

DUETTO, "Cantando un' di" Clari. (First time.) Mdlle. Euphrosyne Parepa and Miss Susanna Cole.

ARIA, "Com' ape ingegnosa" (Tarrare)--Salieri.

(First time.)

Mr. Winn.

SONATA, in Eflat, for 2 Violins and Violoncello (No. 11, Op. 2)----Corelli.

(First time.)

Herr Becker, Herr Ries, and Signor Piatti.

PART II.

GRAND QUARTET, in Eflat major (No. 1), for 2 Violins, Viola and Violoncello-Cherubini. (First time.)

Herr Becker, Herr Ries, Mr. Doyle, and Signor Piatti.

GRAND ARIA, "Se il del mi divide" (Di-done

Abbandonata)-

(First time.)

Mdlle. Euphrosyne Parepa.

VARIATIONS on "Nel cor piii" for Violin alone (First time.)

Herr Becker.

ARIA (Almaviva), "Io son Lindoro" (First time.)

Mr. Tennant.

DUETTO (Almaviva and Bartolo), "O che umor" (First time.)

Mr. TennaDt and Mr. Winn.

TERZETTO (Rosina, Almaviva, and Bartolo),

"Ah chi sa questo suo foglio" (First time.)

Miss Susanna Cole, Mr. Tennant, and Mr. Winn.

QUARTETT, in D major (No. 5), for 2 Violins,

Viola, and Violoncello----

(First time.)

Herr Becker, Herr Ries, Mr. Doyle, and Signor Piatti.

Conductor, Mr. BENEDICT.

Piccini. Paganini. (Barbiere di Siviglia Paesiello) Rossini. Rossini.

Monday. April 9th, 1860.

PROGRAMME, (exclusively selected from the Vocal and Instrumental works of English Composers.) PART L QUARTET, in Gmajor, for 2 Violins, Viola, and Violoncello---Alfred Mellon.

M. Sainton, Herr Ries, Mr. Doyle, and SigDor Piatti.

SONG, "In vain would I forget thee" (Bertha)....-Henry Smart.

Mr. Sims Reeves.

SONG, "The Dew-drop and the Rose"-G. A. Osborne.

Miss Eyles.

SONG, "Rough wind that moanest loud" J. W. Davidson. Mr. Santley. MADRIGAL, "Maidens, never go a-wooing" (Charles n)----Macfarren.

The London Glee and Madrigal Union.

! SONG, "I wander by my dear one's door each night"-----J. L. Nation. Mr. Sims Reeves. SONATA, in Bflat major, for Pianoforte and Violin Dussek.

Mr. Lindsay Sloper, and M. Sainton.

Part n.

TRIO, in E, for Pianoforte. Violin and Violoncello Macfarren.

Mr. Lindsay Sloper, M. Sainton, and Signor Piatti.

GLEE, "By Celia's Arbour"---Horsley.

The London Glee and Madrigal Union.

SONG, "Lovely maiden, keep thy heart for me" M. W. Balfe.

Mr. Sims Reeves. SKETCHES, "The Lake, the Mill-stream, and the Fountain", Pianoforte alone SterndaleBennett Mr. Lindsay Sloper..SONG, "The Bell-Ringer"---Wallace. Mr. Santley.

SONG, "Near Woodstock Town" (Old English Ditty) ----W. Chappell.

Miss Eyles.

GLEE, "Blow, gentle gales"-Bishop.

The London Glee and Madrigal Union.

Conductor, Mr. BENEDICT.

Monday, January 31st, 1870.

PROGRAMME.

PART L

QUARTET, in Eflat, Op. 74, for 2 Violins,

Viola, and Violoncello... *Beethoven.*

MM. Joachim, Straus, L. Ries, and Piatti.

SONG, "Vedrai carino"----*Mozart.*

Miss Blanche Cole. FANTASIA, in Fsharp minor, for Pianoforte alone *Mendelssohn.*

Herr Paner.

Part n.

CHACONNE, for Violin alone---*Bach.*

Herr Joachim.

SONG, "Penitence" *Beethoven.*

Miss Blanche Cole.

TRIO, in C minor, Op. 1, No. 3, for Pianoforte, Violin, and Violoncello--*Beethoven.* MM. Pauer, Joachim, and Fiatti.

Conductor, Mr. ZERBINI.

Monday, January 19th, 1880.

PROGRAMME.

PART L

QUARTET, in F minor, Op. 95, for 2 Violins,

Viola, and Violoncello... *Beethoven.*

Madame Norman-Neruda, MM. L. Ries, Zerbini, and Piatti.

SONG, "Busslied" *Beethoven.*

Mdlle. Anna Schauenburg.

BALLADE, in Aflat, for Pianoforte alone-*Chopin.* Mdlle. Janotha. PART EL SONATA, in D major, for Violin, with Pianoforte accompaniment----*Corelli.*

Madame Norman-Neruda.

SONG, "Schwedisches Lied"---*Geyer.*

Mdlle. Anna Schauenburg.

TRIO, in Bflat, for Pianoforte, Violin, and

Violoncello..... *Mozart.*

Mdlle. Janotha, Madame Norman-Neruda, and Signor Piatti.

Conductor, Mr. ZERBINL

Monday, February 18th, 1891.

PROGRAMME.

PART T.

QUARTET, in C sharp minor, Op. 131, for 2

Violins, Viola, and Violoncello--*Beethoven.*

MM. Ysaye, Marchot, Von Hout, and J. Jacob.

RECITATIVE and ARIA, "Deh vieni, non taidar" (Le Nozze di Figaro)---*Mozart.* Miss Beatrice Spencer. SONATA, in C minor, Op. Ill, for Pianoforte alone------*Beethoven.*

Signer Busoni.

PART II. SONGS:— a. "Air de la Mere-Bobi" (Rose et Colas) *Monsigny.* b. "One Spring Morning"--*£. Nevin.* Miss Beatrice Spencer.

SONATA, in A major, Op. 47, dedicated to

Kreutzer, for Pianoforte and Violin--*Beethoven.*

MM. Busoni and Ysaye.

Accompanist, Mr. HENRY BIRD.

Although the Philharmonic Society is the oldest Musical institution in England, its concerts dating as far back as March, 1813, I have purposely refrained from giving its programmes the pride of place to which their antiquity, apart from their high musical value, fully entities them, for the reason that this Society has until recent years depended upon the support of a select and comparatively small circle of musicians rather than upon that of the general public.

A brief survey of the main achievements of the Society, in their chronological order, will, I trust be sufficiently interesting to condone my sin in thus exceeding the period with which this booklet claims to deal.

The thanks of all of us are due to the Philharmonic Society for having introduced nearly every musician of note to the English public during the first half of the last century. It was under their aegis that Cherubini made his first English appearance, in 1815, when two overtures of his were performed, while in 1820 Spohr played his Dramatic Scena for Violin, and a Duet for Violin and Harp with his wife; a symphony of his was also performed in the same year.

Conducting at the time was totally unlike that which obtains at the present day. The conductor used to sit at a pianoforte, and when anything went wrong he touched the notes on the piano or gave the cue with his hands. This had hithero been the practice at the Philharmonic, whose concerts Clementi was the first to conduct, and it was not till

Spohr's visit in 1820 that the use of the baton was first introduced into England. In his autobiography he refers to the incident in the following terms:—

"1 resolved, when my turn came to direct, to attempt to remedy this defective system. At the morning rehearsal on the day I was to conduct, I took my stand with a score at a separate music-desk in front of the orchestra, drew my directing baton from my coat pocket, and gave the signal to begin. Quite alarmed at such novel procedure, some of the directors would have protested against it; but when I besought them to grant me at least one trial, they became pacified. The triumph of the baton as a timegiver was decisive, and no one was seen again seated at the piano during the performance of symphonies and overtures."

I The Society were also responsible for the appearance of Moscheles in 1821, when he played a manuscript Concerto of his own, and created a sensation by his *bravura* playing.

In 1825 Beethoven wrote his Ninth Symphony for the Philharmonic, receiving a sum of £50 for the composition.

In 1826 Weber conducted the third concert of the season, and evoked great enthusiasm.

In 1827 Liszt, who was then sixteen years old, made his first appearance in England, playing one of Hummel's Concertos.

In 1829 Mendelssohn, at the age of twenty, conducted a manuscript Symphony of his own at one of these concerts, this being his first introduction to the English public.

In 1831 Hummel appeared, also for the first time in this country, and played his *Fantaisie Characteristique sur un Air Indien ef Oberon.*

In 1833 Sterndale Bennett, then a student of seventeen, made his ddbut as a composer and pianist in his Concerto in Eflat.

In 1836 Thalberg made his first English appearance, playing his Second Caprice for Piano and Orchestra.

In 1842 Joachim, when only thirteen years of age, played the Beethoven Concerto from memory, a feat almost unparalleled at the time.

In 1846 Mendelssohn played Beethoven's Concerto in G. This was his last public appearance in England, for he died in November of the same year.

Costa was nominated conductor in 1846, and retained the post until 1854.

In 1852 the directors invited Berlioz to conduct some of his own compositions, but these performances were not particularly successful, his works being generally condemned by the musical critics.

In 1854 the first performance of a Schumann Symphony took place, also without success.

When Costa resigned, the directors entrusted Richard Wagner with the conductorship for the season of 1855. He was then quite unknown in England, and met with very little success, the Press attacking him as one man.

This year was further notable for the first appearance in England of Madame Schumann, who played Beethoven's Concerto in Eflat.

In 1857 Rubinstein first faced an English audience, playing his own Concerto in G.

These are achievements of which any institution might well boast, and when one remembers that, but for the Philharmonic Society, the appearance in England of many of these illustrious musicians would have been greatly retarded, and Beethoven's Ninth Symphony might never have been written, one realises what a great claim it has to the gratitude of the whole musical world. Surely this claim will be allowed, and adequate support given to this, the very oldest of all English musical institutions, so that when it celebrates its centenary six years hence, it may be in as flourishing a condition as at any previous point in its lengthy and useful career.

The subjoined programmes bring the work of the Society up to a comparatively recent date:— PHILHARMONIC SOCIETY.

Monday, April 20th, 1857.
PART I.
SINFONIA, in Eflat, No. 8---*Haydn.*

ARIA, "Di militari onori" (Jessonda)--*Spohr.*
Signor Belletti.
CONCERTO, in D minor, for Pianoforte-*Mendelssohn.*
Miss Arabella Goddard.
RECITATIVE, "EiT edler Held", ARIA, "Du, mein Heil" (Oberon)-*Weber.*
Madame Rudersdorff. OVERTURE, "Euryanthe"-*Weber.* PART IL SINFONIA, in D, No. 2----*Beethoven.* CONCERTINO, "En forme d'une scene chantante", for Violoncello-*F.A.Kummer.*
Signor Piatti.
DUETTO, "Quel sepolcro" (Agnese)--*Paer.*
Madame Rudersdorff and Signor Belletti.
OVERTURE, "Les Deux Journees"--*Ckerubini.*
Conductor, Professor STERNDALE BENNETT.
Monday, March 11th, 1867.
PART L
SYMPHONY, in C minor, No. 1---*Mendelssohn.* RECITATIVE ed "Costanza! presso al tuo bel ciglio", ARIA, "Ah! tral timor"
(II Seraglio) *Mozari.*
Mr. W. H. Cummings OVERTURE, "The Naiades"---*W.S.Bennett.* ROMANZA, "L'ombrosa notte vien" (Matilda) *Hummel.*
Miss Louisa Pyne.
CONCERTO, No. 9, for Violin---*Spohr.*
Herr Joachim.
PART K SYMPHONY, in A, No. 7----*Beethoven.* DUO, "Pourguoi m'evitezvous"? (La Reine de Saba) *Gounod.* (First time of performance in this country.)
Miss Louisa Pyne and Mr. W. H. Cummings.
OVERTURE, "Les Abencerages"--*Cherubini.*
Conductor, Mr. W. G. CUSINS.
Thursday, February 22nd, 1877.
PROGRAMME.
OVERTURE, "Melusine"----*Mendelssohn.*
CONCERTO, in Aminor, Op. 16, for Pianoforte *Ed. Grieg.*
Mr. Ed. Dannreuther.
AIR, "Where'er you walk" (Semele)--*Handel.*

Mr. W. H. Cummings.
SYMPHONY, in C minor, No. 5---*Beethoven.* ODE, "Dalla tore sua romita" (Saffo)--*Gounod.*
Madame Edith Wynne.
DRAMATIC CONCERTO, "Scena Cantante", for Violin------*Spohr.*
Mr. Henry Holmes.
DUETTO, "Da te lontan piu vivere"--*W. G.Cusins.*
Madame Edith Wynne and Mr. W. H. Cummings.
OVERTURE, "Oberon"-*Weber.*
Conductor. Mr. W. G. CUSINS.
Thursday, March 10th, 1887.
PROGRAMME.
PART I.
OVERTURE, "Ruy Bias"----*Mendelssohn.*
RECITATIVE and AIR, "Oh River, dear river"
(Nadeshda)--*A.GoringThomas.* (First time at these concerts.)
Madame Valleria.
CONCERTO.Jin Aminor, for Pianoforte-*Schumann.*
Madame Schumann.
PART II. SYMPHONY, in E minor, No. 4---*Brahms.* (First time at these concerts.) LIEDER — a) "Winterlied"----*Mendelssohn.* b) "Widmung"--*Schumann.*
Madame Valleria. (Accompanied by Signor Bisaccia.) FINALE (Perpetuum mobile) from Suite in F *Moszkowski.* (Composed expressly for this Society.)
Conductor. Mr. C.EORGE MOUNT.
Thursday, May 30th, 1907.
PROGRAMME.
OVERTURE, "Butterfly's Ball"---*Cowen.*
CONCERTO, in A, for Pianoforte--*Grieg.*
Frl. Johanne Stockmarr.
SONGS:—a) Scena from "Die Walkiire"-*Wagner.* b) "Marriage des Roses"--*Cesar Franck.* M. Georges Mauguiere.
CONCERTO, in E, for Violin---*Mendelssohn.* SYMPHONY, "The Pastoral"---*Beethoven.*
Conductor, Dr. FREDERICK COWEN.

My last programme is that of one of my own Pianoforte Recitals given at the St. James's Hall and regarded at the time as a very original and daring experiment:— ST. JAMES'S HALL *PIANOFORTE RECITAL.* Wednesday Afternoon, February 2nd, 1881. PROGRAMME. SONATA in

Bflat, Op. 106---*Beethoven,* SONATA in Aflat, Op. 39----*Weber.* SONATA in F minor, Op. 5---*Brahms.* SONATA in B minor *Liszt.*

Mr. OSCAR BERINGER.

PRESENT AND FUTURE OF THE PIANOFORTE. IN bringing this short fifty years' history of the pianoforte up to date, I shall confine myself to a brief statement of facts, without any attempt at elaborate comment. I can scarcely be blamed for adopting this policy, since it is obvious that, in dealing with contemporary happenings, the lack of perspective makes the task of criticism and comparison equally difficult and unenviable.

The most eminent of the foreign pianists of the present day are:—Paderewski, Busoni, Pachmann, Vianna da Motta, Riesler, Moritz Rosenthal, Pugno, Godowsky, and Sapellnikoff; while the fair sex is strongly represented by such talented artistes as Theresa Carreno, Backer Grondal, Sophie Menter, Clothilde Kleeberg, and Marie Stockmarr. Nearly all of these pay frequent professional visits to this country.

In England we have at the present day a greater number of good pianists, real music-lovers who take their art seriously, than has ever before been the case. The most prominent of those who have been before the public for some time are Fanny Davies, Agnes Zimmermann, Katherine Goodson, Adelina de Lara, Gertrude Peppercorn, Leonard Borwick, Frederick Dawson, Howard Jones, and Cuthbert Whitemore. These alone make a brave enough showing, but treading close upon their heels is a talented band of younger artists who are now rapidly forcing their way to the front. Such are Adela Verne, Irene Scharrer, Winifred Christie, Marguerite Elzy, Rosamond Ley, Margaret Bennett, Vera Margolies, Arthur Newstead, Marmaduke Barton, York Bowen, Percy Grainger, Felix Swinstead, Meyrick, and Herbert Fryer. To this honours-list I must add the names of Eugen d'Albert and Frederick Lamond, who, though domiciled in Germany, are Englishmen, and worthy in every way to be included.

England may well be proud of her possession of such an array of talent, which it would be hard to equal in any other country; and when one compares the present prosperity of the art with its utter stagnation of fifty years back, one can only be devoutly thankful for the change, and for the factors that have brought that change to pass.

To my mind the two chief causes of this marvellous improvement are, (i) the infinitely better teaching given to the student, and, (2) the excellent system of musical examinations which now obtains throughout the country.

It would perhaps be invidious for me to single out the most eminent pianoforte-teachers by name; suffice it to say that there is at the present moment an extraordinarily large number of earnest and thoroughly competent English professors, whose methods compare favourably with those of the best teachers in other countries, as indeed is proved by the excellent playing of their pupils, in private as well as in public.

To the Associated Board of the Royal Academy and Royal College of Music is due the utmost credit for having instituted a system of musical examinations which embraces the whole of the British Empire. Much has been said both for and against examinations as a real test of the candidates' skill, but there can be no doubt (as an examiner for the Association from its inception I can claim some authority for the statement) that the result of these examinations at least has been a marked improvement in the ability of the examinees. When I recall the playing to which I had to listen in 1890, the first year of these examinations, and contrast it with what I hear now, it seems almost incredible to me that so great a change for the better has been effected in such a short time.

Much of the value of these examinations lies in the fact that they force a would-be candidate to learn to play good music and to play it correctly, thus at the same time testing the teacher's capacity to the full; they implant a healthy spirit of emulation into the hearts of the competitors, and give them a definite object fot which to work.

More important even than these are the examinations for the degree of Licentiateship of the Royal Academy of Music and that of Associateship of the Royal College of Music. For teachers these degrees have become almost a necessity—they are the musical "hallmark" which guarantees the possessor to have the knowledge, practical and theoretical, necessary for a competent teacher. A practical proof that the importance of being able to put L. R. A. M. or A. R. C. M. after one's name is recognised, is the yearly increase in the candidature for the qualifying examinations.

Further aid towards progress has been lent by the competitive musical festivals, Eistedfodds, etc. I have adjudicated at many of these in various parts of the country, and have invariably found that the standard of playing steadily improves year by year.

These, in my opinion, are the prime causes of the extraordinary advance made in the art of pianforteplaying of recent years, and it is most gratifying to reflect that, with these causes continuing in active existence, it is practically impossible for the ball of progress ever to stop rolling.

As far as compositions for the pianoforte are concerned, Russia is indisputably first amongst the nations; for what other country can lay claim to an equal number of talented composers to compare with Tschaikowsky, Glazounow, Arensky, Rachmaninoff, Liapunow, Blumenfeld, Scriabine, and Cesar Cui?

, Scandinavia runs Russia very close with Grieg, Sinding, Sibelius, Sjorgen, and many others.

There are not many composers of Polish and Bohemian nationality, of whom the most prominent are Paderewski, Moszkowski, and Novacek.

Italy has Martucci, Sgambati, Esposito, who lives in Dublin, and Albanesi, who lives in London.

Of late years German composers of the highest rank have left pianofortemusic severely alone: Richard Strauss, in his earlier compositions, Max Reger, whom I confess I do not understand,

Xaver Scharwenka, and some very minor satellites, complete the scanty tale.

France has recently gone in for what, for lack of a better term, I must call the impressionist style. This school writes programme music, pure—but by no means simple, and portrays emotions by a happy disregard of the rules of harmony. Even composers of repute, like Vincent d'Indy and Debussy, must plead guilty to this charge. Faure is much less of an impressionist, and frequently writes really beautiful melodies, while to Madame Chaminade we owe some *salon* music of real merit.

In glancing at the more strictly classical composers of the present day in England, I have a friendly bone to pick with the Seniors. What has poor Miss Pianoforte done to them, that she should be shunned and neglected, like a poor little wall-flower at a dance?

They have one and all laid themselves open to this charge. Sir Alexander Mackenzie has, during a considerable number of years, only written one pianoforte work, to wit his excellent Concerto for that instrument. Since his very earliest attempts, Sir Hubert Parry has entirely neglected this branch of composition. Sir Charles Stanford has recently written three pieces on Dante's *Inferno,* but this, I believe, is his grand total. Elgar has only contributed a few unimportant trifles, and Cowen has been equally parsimonious.

The Juniors, I am glad to say, have been more gallant, and have paid homage to the wall-flower. For them

she is the belle of the ball. They have written some admirable pianoforte compositions, including such excellent works as McEwen's Sonata, the Sonata by Dale, and the many charming works of Eugen d'Albert, York Bowen, Farjeon, Paul Corder, Percy Pitt, Swinstead, and the rest.

This is as it should be, for while such men as those I have mentioned flourish in this country, Miss Pianoforte and her many lovers will also continue flourishing, in spite of the incursions of the pianola and various other types of music-making machinery.

I must now bring this *resume* of my fifty years' experience of pianoforte-teaching and playing to a close. In it I have endeavoured to give an absolutely unbiassed account of the progress of pianoforte-music in this country, and to trace, step by step, the enormous improvement that has taken place, here and elsewhere, during that 72 Fifty Years' Experience of Pianoforte Teaching and Playing.

period. Sets-back there have been, and must always be, for the path of true art, like that of true love, never yet ran smooth; but, with music playing a more and more important part in the life and culture of the nations of the world, I dare to say that that progress will continue uninterruptedly, and that the pianoforte will never lose its present proud position as one of the most valuable factors in the education of humanity at large *The End.* GREAT SYSTEMS OF INSTRUCTION. BERINGER, Oscar. For the

Pianoforte.

"May be recommended as practically the best in existence." *The Lady.*

"Among the mass of instruction books now extant, we know of no other superior to this." *Musical News.*

Beringer's Celebrated Scale and Arpeggio Manual.. net 2/Beringer's Daily Technical Studies net 5

These great modern works, which reach the culminating point in methodized technical ins ruction, may be seen and examined at any good musicseller's in the United Kingdom. Descriptive prospectuses and booklet will be sent gratis and post-free on application.

Practical Teaching material. Pianoforte.

H. Germer. In four books each net 2/3 d.

(Bosworth Edition Nos. 3 to 6.)

W.Schwarz. Six progressive Elementary Albums each net 1/ (Bosworth Edition Nos. 355 ami i07 to 411.)

Folk Songs &c. Can be used with any Tutor. Highly recommended.

Being the most celebrated educational music of the Great Masters of each Instrument, edited, analysed, and progressively arranged by the foremost modern technical experts. These collections are of the utmost value and utility to Professors of the Pianoforte, saving them much time and trouble.

A. Seppings.

Tiny Tunes for Tiny Tots. An absolutely reasonable Pianoforte Tutor or Guide for quite young children.

Lightning Source UK Ltd.
Milton Keynes UK
UKHW032018070619

344049UK00007B/673/P